Reasons for Rebellion

Some Other Titles From New Falcon Publications

Aha! The Sevenfold Mystery of the Ineffable Love	**Aleister Crowley**
An Insider's Guide to Robert Anton Wilson	**Eric Wagner**
Bio-Etheric Healing	**Trudy Lanitis**
Undoing Yourself With Energized Meditation and Other Devices, Secrets of Western Tantra: The Sexuality of the Middle Path, Dogma Daze	**Christopher S. Hyatt, Ph.D.**
Rebels & Devils; The Psychology of Liberation	**Edited by Christopher S. Hyatt, Ph.D.**
Aleister Crowley's Illustrated Goetia, Sex Magic, Tantra & Tarot: The Way of the Secret Lover, Taboo: Sex, Religion & Magick	**C. S. Hyatt, Ph.D., and DuQuette**
Pacts With The Devil, Urban Voodoo: A Beginner's Guide to Afro-Caribbean Magic	**Jason Black and Christopher S. Hyatt, Ph.D.**
The Psychopath's Bible	**Christopher S. Hyatt, Ph.D., and Jack Willis**
Ask Baba Lon	**Lon Milo DuQuette**
Aleister Crowley and the Treasure House of Images	**J.F.C. Fuller, Aleister Crowley, Lon Milo DuQuette and Nancy Wasserman**
Enochian Sex Magic and How To Workbook	**Aleister Crowley, Lon Milo DuQuette and Christopher S. Hyatt, Ph.D.**
Enochian World of Aleister Crowley	**DuQuette and Aleister Crowley**
Info-Psychology, Neuropolitique, The Game of Life, What Does WoMan Want?	**Timothy Leary, Ph.D.**
Paganism in Christian Holidays	**J. M. Wheeler**
Nonlocal Nature: The Eight Circuits of Consciousness	**James A. Heffernan**
Numbers Their Meaning and Magic, Vol I, and Vol II, Zodiacal Symbology and It's Planetary Power, Book One and Book Two	**Isidore Kozminsky**
on What is	**Ja Wallin**
Rebellion, Revolution and Religiousness	**Osho**
Reichian Therapy: A Practical Guide for Home Use	**Dr. Jack Willis**
Shaping Formless Fire, Seizing Power, Taking Power, The Magick in the Music and Other Essays	**Stephen Mace**
The Illuminati Conspiracy: The Sapiens System	**Donald Holmes, M.D.**
The Philosophy of Numbers, Vol I and Vol II, Nature's Symphony, Lessons in Number Vibration	**Mrs. L. Dow Balliett**
The Secret Inner Order Rituals of the Golden Dawn	**Pat Zalewski**
The Why, Who, and What of Existence	**Vlad Korbel**
Steamo Goes to Havana, The Social Epidemic of Child Abuse	**Michael Miller, M.Ed., M.S., Ph.D.**
Woman's Orgasm: A Guide to Sexual Satisfaction	**Benjamin Graber, M.D., and Georgia Kline-Graber, R.N.**
Zingara Art of Divinition	**Ana Calaroni**

Titles by J. Marvin Spiegelman, Ph.D.
A Modern Jew in Search of Soul
Buddhism and Jungian Psychology
Catholicism and Jungian Psychology
Hinduism and Jungian Psychology
Mysticism, Psychology and Oedipus - A Small Gem
Protestanism and Jungian Psychology
Psychotherapy and Religion at the Millennium and Beyond
Psychotherapy as a Mutual Process
Reich, Jung, Regardie & Me - The Unhealed Healer
Rider, Haggard, Henry Miller & I - The Unpublished Writer
Sufism, Islam and Jungian Psychology
The Knight - A Small Gem
The Nymphomaniac
The Quest - Further Adventures in the Unconscious
The Tree of Life - Paths in Jungian Individuation
The Wisdom of J. Marvin Speigelman Vol. I - Selected Writings
The Wisdom of J. Marvin Speigelman Vol. II - Psychology and Religion

Other Titles by Dr. Israel Regardie

A Garden of Pomegranates
A Practical Guide to Geomantic Divination - A Small Gem
Attract and Use Healing Energy - A Small Gem
Be Yourself - A Guide to Relaxation and Health
Ceremonial Magic
Dr. Israel Regardie's Definitive Work on Aleister Crowley,
   The Eye In The Triangle
Healing Energy, Prayer and Relaxation
How To Make and Use Talismans - A Small Gem
Israel Regardie's The Foundations of Practical Magick
My Rosicrucian Adventure
Mysticism, Psychology and Oedipus - A Small Gem
Practical Magick - A Small Gem
Teachers of Fulfillment
The Art and Meaning of Magic - A Small Gem
The Body-Mind Connection, A Path to Well-Being - A Small Gem
The Complete Golden Dawn System of Magic
The Complete Golden Dawn System of Magic Book 1 - Ltd. Edition
The Complete Golden Dawn System of Magic Book 2 - Ltd. Edition
The Complete Golden Dawn System of Magic - The Black Edition
The Eye in the Triangle: An Interpretation of Aleister Crowley
The Golden Dawn Audio CDs, Vol. 1, Vol. 2, and Vol. 3
The Legend of Aleister Crowley
The Magic of Israel Regardie
The Middle Pillar
The Philosopher's Stone
The Portable Complete Golden Dawn System of Magic
The Tree of Life
The Wisdom of Israel Regardie - Vol. I
   Selected Introductions, Prefaces and Forewords
The Wisdom of Israel Regardie - Vol. II
   Selected Essays and Commentaries
The Wisdom of Israel Regardie - Vol. III
   Selected Articles, Introductions, Prefaces and Forewords
What You Should Know About the Golden Dawn
Wilhelm Reich, His Theory And Techniques
Aha! (Dr. Israel Regardie and Aleister Crowley)
Roll Away The Stone/The Herb Dangerous
   (Dr. Israel Regardie and Aleister Crowley)

MANY OF OUR TITLES AVAILABLE ON KINDLE!
Please visit our website at http://www.newfalcon.com

Copyright ©New Falcon Publications 2024

All rights reserved. No part of this book, in part or in whole, may be reproduced, transmitted, or utilized, in any form or by any means, electronic or mechanical, including photocopying, recording, or by any information storage and retrieval system, without permission in writing from the publisher, except for brief quotations in critical articles, books and reviews.

ISBN 13: 978-1-56184-528-6

ISBN 10: 1-56184-528-0

First New Falcon Publications Edition 2024

The paper used in this publication meets the minimum requirements of the American National Standard for Permanence of Paper for Printed Library Materials Z39.48-1984

Printed in USA

NEW FALCON PUBLICATIONS
2046 Hillhurst Avenue
Los Angeles, CA 90027
www.newfalcon.com
email: info@newfalcon.com

Reasons for Rebellion

Preface by
Lon Milo Duquette

Introduction by
Jeff Mandon

Timothy Leary, Ph.D.
Eric Gullichsen
Robert Anton Wilson
Dr. Israel Regardie
Richard Kaczynski, Ph.D.
Dr. William S. Hyatt, Ph.D.
James Wasserman
Chic and S. Tabatha Cicero
Lon Milo DuQuette
Peter Conte
Osho (Bhagwan Shree Rejneesh)
Steven Heller, Ph.D.
Dr. Jack S. Willis
Jeff Mandon
Wayne Saalman

NEW FALCON PUBLICATIONS
LOS ANGELES, CALIFORNIA, U.S.A.

Table of Contents

Preface *Lon Milo DuQuette*	ix
Introduction *Jeff Mandon*	xix
Taboo and Transformation in the Words of Aleister Crowley *Richard Kaczynski, Ph.D.*	1
Basic Principles of Magic *Dr. Israel Regardie*	15
Pulling Liberty's Teeth *James Wasserman*	27
Rebellion Is The Biggest "YES" Yet *Osho (Bhagwan Shree Rejneesh)*	51
Twenty-Two Alternatives to Involuntary Death *Timothy Leary Ph.D. and Eric Gullichsen*	69
Theurgia Liberatio: Magic As Divine Liberation *Chic and S. Tabatha Cicero*	93
Team Psychopath *Peter Conte*	115

Devil Be My God 　*Lon Milo DuQuette*	125
Breaking Trance 　*Steven Heller, Ph.D.*	129
The Black Art of Psychotherapy 　*Dr. Jack S. Willis*	131
Another Bedtime Story *Dr. William S. Hyatt, Ph.D.*	141
Greek Magic *from Ceremonial Magic* 　*Dr. Israel Regardie*	149
Introduction to The Dream Illuminati A Global Revolution Takes Wing by Wayne Saalman 　*Robert Anton Wilson*	181
Excerpt from 　*CRUMBS...and Other Things I've Followed Home* *Jeff Mandon*	195
Angels, Devils, Spiritual Rebels 　*Wayne Saalman*	223
Authors	239

Preface

Lon Milo DuQuette

*Unthinking respect for authority
is the greatest enemy of truth.*
–Albert Einstein

Do what thou wilt shall be the whole of the Law.

My involvement in this unique and historic publication project began in late 1995 when my friend (and co-author on four book projects[1]), Alan R. Miller (aka Christopher S. Hyatt), called to say he wanted to take me out to dinner. I was a little hesitant to accept because we had a bit of a falling out a couple of years earlier and were speaking to each other as infrequently as possible. He invited me to choose the time and place so I picked a time and suggested The Arches in Newport Beach, one of the oldest (and most expensive) restaurants in the area. He said, "Done."

While drinking the best martinis in southern California we tried to recall exactly what had happened to sour our relationship. It didn't take long for us to remember that it was a boisterous night of being ruthlessly frank with each other–a slurred debate full of mutual observations of personal shortcomings spawned by too many of these damned martinis. After a silent moment or two of embarrassed reflection, we chose to sip white wine through the rest of the dinner.

---

[1] *Enochian World of Aleister Crowley, The Way of the Secret Lover, Aleister Crowley's Illustrated Goetia,* and *Taboo: Sex Religion and Magick.* All from New Falcon Publications.

We weren't meeting, however, to reminisce or patch up our friendship. He wanted to talk to me about a new project–an anthology of short works by some of the most controversial writers of the twentieth century including Dr. Timothy Leary, Robert Anton Wilson, Osho (Bhagwan Shree Rajneesh), and a host of other radical minds of the day.

It was a wonderful idea, and I told him so. After all, how many publishers go out of the way to present ideas that are viewed by the majority of our neighbors as being rebellious, obscene, subversive, blasphemous, insane, and dangerous? The market for such a work is very small. I was flattered and a bit surprised when I was asked to contribute an article. I enthusiastically agreed. I had just the thing for the book.[2]

Compared with most of the other writers in this unique work my credentials might seem rather anemic. I was born in a pleasant suburb of Los Angeles in the late 1940s, raised in a pleasant (but woefully unconscious) small town in Nebraska, and, until my sophomore year in high school, never seriously labored in my mind about politics, religion, the nature of consciousness or the meaning (or the meaningless) of life.

The war in Vietnam (and the very real possibility that I would be drafted to fight and perhaps die for something I really didn't understand) served to underscore the importance of being awake while my classmates quietly sleep-marched into body bags. I had no idea where to begin this waking up process, but I knew I would have to do something, and fast. As it turned out, it would be something I decided *not* to do that put me on the fateful road to rebellion.

I was pondering my predicament as I took my seat in the

---

[2] *See* Devil Be My God.

high school auditorium and prepared to endure a patriotic convocation sponsored by the American Legion, and featuring greedy recruiters from the various branches of the Armed Services there to hungrily harvest a fresh crop of cannon fodder. Naturally, the convocation began with a color guard of Boy Scouts trooping the American flag to center stage. As if we were now in the presence of the Holy Grail, the unseen voice of Principal Boyd serenely ordered the assembly to stand up and recite the "Pledge of Allegiance to the Flag of the United States of America."

Now, please understand that I had always been proud to be an American and loved the principles (as much as a high school sophomore understood them) of our republic, and all those "freedoms" that I knew were not enjoyed by citizens of many other countries around the world. But the Pledge of Allegiance to the *Flag* had disturbed me from the moment I was bullied into taking part in the exercise in elementary school. Today something snapped. Today I said to myself 'fuck no!' I remained seated and silent during the pledge. No one seemed to notice…but I was wrong.

Later in the day I was stopped in the hall by Mr. Brown, a new social studies teacher from Colorado who had just been hired to replace his recently deceased predecessor. He said he noticed that I had not stood for the Pledge of Allegiance and asked me why. I told him I thought the whole things was stupid and that I resented the whole assembly's attempt to suck my naive classmates into a stupid-sounding war. I fully expected to get a lecture on what a nasty, unpatriotic little bastard I was. Instead, I got a warm smile and an invitation to visit him at his apartment after school.

Over cigarettes and coffee I learned a history of Vietnam conflict that I'd never heard before–a history that the rest of the world seemed to already know. I learned that there was a bigger world out there. I learned that there were many Americans, including Senators and Congressmen, who felt that our involvement in the war was a very un-American thing to do.

In the months that followed I received a world-class education in radical politics. I gathered a small cadre of my misfit friends to join me in these afternoon sessions with Comrade Brown. I started to collect anti-war buttons and bumper stickers, took a short correspondence course in draft counseling, and the dawn of my Junior year was putting it to use teaching lunch hour sessions in how to legally and illegally avoid the draft. This naturally brought down upon me the scorn of the school administration. I was expelled twice—once for refusing to cut my hair, the second time for the outrageously inappropriate charge of "sedition." "Sedition!" For high school draft counseling! Only in Nebraska. A couple of letters from the local Episcopal minister friend in the ACLU got me back in class in short order, but I was branded a cowardly and unpatriotic communist traitor.

By my senior year I was a card carrying rebel. I joined the *Student Peace Union*, the *Young People's Socialist League*, and the *Students for a Democratic Society*. To all but a couple of girlfriends and a close circle of fellow travelers, Lon the rebel had now become Lon the devil and the most despised student in Columbus High School. I loved it.

When it came time for me to register myself for the draft, I appeared at the Selective Service office sporting a green beret with a large "Fuck the Draft" button pinned front and center. I also carried with me a letter dated 1950 from the California doctor who originally diagnosed my Perthes hip disease. It read, "Lonnie cannot exercise below the waist." I brutally intimidated the sweet little wheelchair-bound lady at the SS office threatening that if I weren't classified 4-F or I-Y, I would claim Conscientious Objector status and cause so much trouble there would be hundreds of boys in town who would want to do the same thing. It was a ridiculous threat, but since World War I no one in Columbus, Nebraska ever talked to the Draft Board like that.[3]

Then one afternoon in the spring of 1966 I was searching for cigarettes in the drawer of our living room hutch when I discovered a letter from the U.S. Department of Justice in Washington D.C. It was addressed to my mother and included the address and telephone number of the FBI field office in Omaha and the name of an agent for her to contact. Mom was at work so I confronted my father.

The poor man was already barrel-chested and weak from the emphysema. He moved to the couch and started to clean his pipe and nervously tried to talk with me between carefully planned breaths.

"Your mother's worried about you. She thinks you're getting in with some pretty dangerous people. Her cronies at work told her she was being silly but she went ahead and wrote to the FBI. That's the letter she got back. She's already called the Omaha office and told them everything she thinks she knows."

I asked if he had heard her conversation, and he said, "Only the part where she told them that you've fallen in with Communists and that they were teaching you to hate your mother."

We both laughed.

---

[3] I don't know if the threat worked because immediately upon graduation I moved to California. Mail from Selective Service followed me for a while, but I just ignored them and threw them all away unopened. Finally the letters stopped coming. Could it have been that easy for everyone?

I still couldn't fathom what possessed her to do such a thing. I recalled only one occasion when my mother and I ever discussed politics. I drew her a picture of a bird with its wings spread to illustrate the various degrees of philosophies between the extreme left and the extreme right wings of American politics. It was a pleasant conversation (I thought) and pinpointed where FDR were located on the wings and where Barry Goldwater and Lyndon Johnson were located on the big bird. I certainly didn't espouse any subversive or un-American sentiments. I guess the big bird just freaked her out.

Now she was freaking me out, because as innocent as my activities were, from the point of view of a wartime FBI investigation my activities might make me at least *appear* to be a person of interest.

I had taken a summer job delivering broken television sets to an Omaha electronics shop for repair. Each trip I had to wait there, sometimes up to five hours, before returning the 90 miles home with the repaired units. All that time in the big city enabled me to make contact with my urbane comrades in the peace movement, including several Episcopal priests and a Unitarian minister who introduced me to the aging former president of a large international labor union. This man, who had a son my age, was the most interesting character I had ever met. He was at the time an active member of the Progressive Labor Party, but for years was an organizer for the Communist Party U.S.A. He had pictures of himself with Cisco Houston and Woody Guthrie and Pete Seeger and the Weavers; he knew Gus Hall; he'd been shot in the back by strikebreakers in Dearborn, bitten by dogs in Selma, and jailed in Mississippi with Martin Luther King. I couldn't wait for Saturdays so I could visit this delightful page of walking history. I am sure if anybody was a target for domestic surveillance in those dark years it was my colorful commie mentor. But I was harmless enough. Nothing ever came from my involvement with the movement except a Washington dossier marked *Kids-so-wild-their-mothers-turn-em-in* or one for Mom labeled *Mothers-so-crazy-they-turn-in-their-kids*.

In the spring of 1966 I graduated from high school and instantly packed up and drove my blue 1960 VW van back to my Southern California birthplace and pretended to go to college. I registered at Orange Coast College of Costa Mesa. Officially, my major was Drama, but my real major was 'the 60s.' I immediately linked up with the local SDS whose off campus headquarters was a large two story old house in Costa Mesa.

Expecting to find the same kind of somber-faced, but work-shirted denizens of the new Left that populated the University of Nebraska, I instead was greeted by a cadre of some of the most beautiful young people that I had ever seen–surfer boys with sandy blonde locks, and the bra-less hippie goddesses with long straight hair and voices like Joan Baez. I was in teenage rebel heaven. I presented them with a homemade Viet Cong flag. They presented me with a pipe-load of hashish and an invitation to a lecture by the greatest (then) living rebel and devil of them all, Dr. Timothy Leary. My rebel life was about to take a radical turn…inward. But that is another story for another time.[4] I believe that it is safe to say that Dr. Leary's influence played a significant role in shaping the lives, characters, attitudes, and ideas of the majority of the individuals who have contributed to this unique and historic publication.

---

[4] DuQuette, Lon Milo. *My Life With The Spirits*. Weiser Books: Boston, 1999.

In 1980, I and members of the O.T.O.[5] lodge in Newport Beach decided it was time that Dr. Leary received some kind of award–a token of appreciation for his influence upon the evolving consciousness of humanity. We named our award after one of the most infamous rebels and devils of them all, Adam Weisphaupt, the notorious founder of the Bavarian Illuminati. The plaque was laser etched on brass and mounted on heavy walnut. It was framed by the classic image of the Egyptian Goddess Nuit.

The inscription read:

O.T.O.
PEACE   TOLERANCE   TRUTH
SALUTATION ON ALL POINT OF THE TRIANGLE
Do what thou wilt shall be the whole of the Law.
THE GUILD OF ADVANCED THOUGHT   (G∴ O∴ A∴ T∴)
of
HERU-RA-HA LODGE O.T.O.
is honored to present to
DR. TIMOTHY LEARY
THE FIRST ANNUAL
ADAM WEISHAUPT ILLUMINATI AWARD
In recognition of incalculable service to Humanity and others. Because of his inspired research and courageous example, Dr. Leary Is directly responsible for raising the consciousness of our planet.
"YOUR ONLY ALLEGIANCE IS TO LIFE"
Love is the law, love under will.
Given this 11th day of July 1980 E.V.

---

[5] Ordo Templi Orientis (Order of the Temple of the East, or the Order of Oriental Templars) is an international fraternal and religious organization founded at the beginning of the 20th century. Originally it was intended to be modeled after and associated with Freemasonry, but under the leadership of Aleister Crowley was reorganized as a non-Masonic organization based on the Law of Thelema as its central religious principle. This Law–expressed as "Do what thou wilt shall be the whole of the Law" and "Love is the law, love under will"–was established in 1904 with the dictation of *The Book of the Law*.

After his death, this award was listed among the items sold by the auction house, Christie's in New York. If you are interested, you can still see a picture of it on Christie's website, Lot 13/Sale 8113.

In the years following, our lodge also presented the 'Illuminati Award' to two more rebels whose work grace the pages of this book, Dr. Israel Regardie and Robert Anton Wilson. It is with a great deal of ironic amazement that I find my words bound between the covers of this remarkable book along with this new and dangerous generation of rebels and their counterparts who helped pave the way.

Love is the law, love under will.

Lon Milo DuQuette
Costa Mesa, California, November 15, 2008

Introduction

Jeff Mandon

When I was asked to write this introduction, frankly, I was thrilled; because so many of the authors I had sought to inform my thinking in the midst of my prolonged adolescence (which reached far into my 20s) are included here. I sought them to broaden my mind; to give me another side of things. Some of the thoughts they shared were quite radical; and time has done little to dampen them from being any less radical, nor less relevant. I would read these authors' thoughts and opinions, and share them (ham-handedly) with friends and parents; passing them off as my own just to try them out; to varying degrees of welcome. In short, these authors taught me how to think outside the box; and in the end to think for myself. I gobbled down their thoughts and opinions hungrily, because the long and short of it was that I was in rebellion. I guess I still am to some degree. It wasn't necessarily that I was in rebellion against my parents, or against society. I was in rebellion against myself.

I didn't know it then; I just knew I felt like I was outgrowing my skin and needed to shed it in order to survive and thrive. I was struggling to become myself. Far too often, someone had said to me, "just be yourself and everything will be fine." And I would panic, thinking to myself, "I wouldn't know where to begin." And I honestly didn't.

I knew enough to know that it wasn't my personality self that I wanted to be anymore. In fact, that was exactly what I was trying to get away from, because it was basically formed so much by defense mechanisms I had adopted growing up; and growing up scared; which I believe is becoming more and more prevalent among our youth today. Our society is currently infused with so much fear that it's very difficult for a full-grown adult, no less an adolescent, to avoid taking it in, and taking it in deeply.

They say there are only two emotions: Love and fear. Things like hatred, anger, jealousy, etc. are all fear-based when you really dig down deeply enough. I don't think anybody plans to rebel growing up. I mean it's not like you sit up one day and say, "Oh gee, I think I'll push everyone and anything away from me today that I find irritating or errant." And yet I think everyone; or at least most anyone who is worth knowing in the end, has rebelled at some point in their development.

Rebellion comes from deep inside, and I believe it comes when one's heart wakes. For it is then that you notice that so much of what you have been swallowing up to this point, no longer sits well with you. Your desire for liberty, for freedom; comes from deep inside now; as if it were placed there by God himself. And perhaps it is. For those of us who've answered its call, we know there is a price to be paid for that freedom; for that liberty. The price is rebellion, with all its attendant fallout. There's just no way of avoiding it. It's as if you've been renting an apartment all those years and you suddenly turn the light on one day, realize you are a home owner in fact, and you better start to know a little bit about how the lighting works in your home. How it's wired. What those pipes under the sink are all about.

We begin to explore ourselves inside independently. And many authors contained in this book helped shake me loose. In some ways forced me to spit out the candy I was beginning to choke on, that had been placed in my mouth by others far too long as a way of placating me. Because when you're struggling inside, you need to struggle 'til it's over. The gift you are given for this journey is choice. The ability to respond instead of merely react. When you are cognizant of the fact that you are always in choice, you will realize you are free.

Medicating it away doesn't work. Lord knows, I tried that for years; and by medicating I don't just mean medicine, or even drugs; but drinking, and shopping; gambling, watching mindless TV, reading insipid books; basically doing whatever you can to deny your own depths which can no longer pacify you when the heart is awakened. You certainly can't be happy; and on some level, you know it, if you're running that game. But you're willing to settle for a momentary distraction from your pain. A momentary distraction that you milk and moderate with your given magic substance, hoping you can make it last for years; which you can't.

Once you gain your freedom from your own inner fears, from your own blind spots; once you know, and I mean really know yourself enough that you can work on your defects of character as they arise, honestly and scrupulously; navigate your own way, with the sureness that comes from a deep inner connection. That's freedom in this world. Because in your search within you, you find that it's not all bad news; and after all, isn't it that very fear, that kept you from exploring your inner depths for years?

There is a core of God within each and every one of us. And that spirit is of the light. As God is unalterable, so this part of him inside us follows suit; for it's no meager speck. God is indivisible for he is All, so this part of him inside you is full strength maximum-power God. And that Self is not a stranger to you; and yes, surrounding it there are rings of fear that growing up, met with trauma after trauma that you pushed aside, or buried, or failed to notice altogether managed to be the very source that placed them there. And that's your price of admission in reaching your core Self; your soul. But more often than not, as you explore the scary monsters that those rings of fear represent; you find those horrible faces that have so long frightened you, are just masks. And those rings of fear that kept you at bay for far too long, are just wounded children, scared themselves, who are looking for a way to defend against that mini-crucifixion they experienced.

I honestly think it's healthy to rebel at some point in your life. Rebellion is a journey home. It is the hero's journey. It's Dorothy in Oz. It's Luke Skywalker taking on Darth Vader. The hero journey is always worth exploring, because at any given time multitudes of people are experiencing it. The lucky ones overcome their demons and return heroes; but there are no guarantees. I grew up in the country; not every bird that is pushed out of the nest by its mother learns to fly before it hits the ground; but God bless the ones that do fly. They are role models for us all. The beautiful part is anyone and everyone can be a hero in their own life journey.

It doesn't matter the size of their life in terms of public exposure. You don't need to be on TV to be living at a ten. You can be home gardening and living at a ten. What matters is the striving. The earnest desire to be more and more your true Self.

That moment of crisis when you meet your demons is so vital; but let's face it, it's also very frightening. Something I finally learned, is that the difference between a breakdown and a breakthrough is whether you are spiritually alone or not. It's easy to isolate as you rebel in your youth or even in your adulthood; because it's never too late to become your true core Self, and after all, isn't that the point in the end? You can do it at any age, but if you're smart, young or old, you will not do it alone. A mentor is a beautiful thing; and anyone can be a role model for you; both positive and negative role models are all around us. And in any hero journey there are always friends to help keep you on the path and contribute to the final goal of coming home to yourself. And I do mean the Self that God created; not the one we made up to cover the vulnerability, the desire to love and be loved, honestly and deeply. The very one that seemed to have all those flaws when you're growing up, that in the end, turn out to be all the very qualities that you need to succeed in life; that is if you are going to live a life that recognizes the spiritual Self that is you with equal shrift as that body and mind that is also you. That's the extraordinary thing about becoming your core Self. Everyone around you will tell you how much you're changing, and that will be true; but for you, it will feel as if you are simply becoming your real true Self, more and more. The Self you always were deep inside, but were just too frightened or distracted or faithless to be.

It's all about the voice you listen to inside. Listen to the one that tells you to take heart; that tells you to be honest, especially with yourself. The one that knows there really is such a thing as magic and the truth, because you've heard it and felt it and know it; because your metaphysical and physical self, have told you so. Continue to discipline your mind, so that you release the thoughts of ego, which become more and more identifiable as you grow; and return to the thoughts of God which are your true thoughts. And remember we're not responsible for every ugly, vicious thought that flits through our mind. Don't let that distract you. We are responsible for those thoughts we detain; for those we nurture and cultivate.

Again, it's simply about allowing yourself to be your best Self. Because there is a place of God within you that gives rise to your true Self, your true will, will come to match that of God. For they are literally coming from the same place. Your Sacred Heart. It starts when you ask, "What do I want?" And not satisfied with the answer, you ask instead, "No, what do I *really* want?" And you'll be surprised to find the answer is not shallow or greedy; but one of depth, for its coming from your heart. So, it's more than a shopping list; it's a longing; it's a dream you know you can make come true.

It is our nature to lean on something; and if we do not lean on God in this process, we are very likely to lean on something it would be best we not lean on. Oddly enough, when you lean on God, you actually gain a sense of independence in the world that is grounded and palpable; and people will see it and respond to it.

Whether you agree with them or not, this book is full of individualists; true mavericks. Men and women who went out on a limb, not as a goal, but just to live a life true to themselves; and living in truth is a way of life. Here they share their ideas; their wisdom; their truths. I hope you will find here a little inspiration and clarity. And the great thing is when you come back later to re-read this book you will be struck by wisdom you didn't catch the first time because you weren't at a place yet to utilize it. So, as you change, so does the book. May it help you grow. May it offer something you can take in right now that might change things for the better with you. And if you are stuck, may it inspire a rebellion in you; a Rebellion that will leave you better than you are; better than you thought you could be. Enough said. Go love.

Aleister Crowley (in 1906)
The Father of Modern Western Magick
Born 1875, Died 1947

TABOO AND TRANSFORMATION
IN THE WORK OF ALEISTER CROWLEY
Richard Kacynski, Ph.D.

Spiritual polymorph, sexual omnivore, psychedelic pioneer, and unapologetic social misfit, Aleister Crowely cut a scandalous figure in his Edwardian heyday. He was rediscovered during the counter-cultural revolution of the 1960s and beatified as a pop culture icon, with the groundswell of interest resulting from his renaissance yet to crest. While his detractors are as numerous as his admirers, to dismiss him as a mere hedonist is to ignore the ghost in the machine: As Gerald Yorke, Crowely's friend and *advocatus diabolus*, explained: "Crowley didn't *enjoy* his perversion! He performed them to overcome his horror of them."[1] Yorke's is no disingenuous revisionist memoir. Throughout Crowley's corpus runs of the idea of spiritual transformation by plunging into one's phobias and philias.

The ceremonial magick championed by Crowley and his forebears in the Golden Dawn is, in a nutshell, alchemy: The transformation of one's base character into spiritual gold. Crowley sought to improve upon this High Art by channeling human nature's most powerful drives into a form of sexual alchemy. His rationale, while not using this language, boils down to a simple thesis: If psychological triggers can precipi-

---

[1] Fuller, Jeanne Overton. The Magical Dilemma of Victor Neuburg. London: W.H. Allen, 1965, p. 244.

tate spiritual change, then the taboos socially programmed into us can act as triggers for major spiritual transformation. Thus, Crowley spent his life probing the impulses against which guilt, sin or plain common sense dissuaded most.

This behavior found its earliest expression in what Crowley admits is a defining moment of his childhood:

> I must have been about 6 years old. I was capering around my father during a walk through the meadows. He pointed out a branch of nettles in the corner of the field, close to the gate (I can see it quite clearly today!) and told me that if I touched them they would sting. Some word, gesture, or expression of mine caused him to add: Would you rather be told, or learn by experience? I replied, instantly, I would rather learn by experience. Suiting the action to the word, I dashed forward, plunged in the clump, and learnt.
>
> This incident is the key to the puzzle of my character.[1]

From there, the exploration of ill-advised impulses became a constant quest. Thanks to his fundamentalist upbringing in the Plymouth Brethren faith, an abundance of taboos presented themselves. Simply reading the wrong book was a potential misstep for the young Crowley. By his teenage years, he had discovered the "Three Evil Kings," i.e., Drin-King, Smo-King and Wan-King.

By the time Crowley entered Trinity College, he understood the hazards of gratuitous sensuality. His second book, the notorious *White Stains* (1898), emulated the Decadent art and literature of his social circle. Critics, then as well as today, twittered at such suggestive titles as "A Ballad of Passive

---

[1] Crowley, Aleister. Chapter LVII. Beings I Have Seen with My Physical Eye. *Magick Without Tears*. New Jersey: Thelema Publishing Co., 1954; rpt. Tempe, AZ: New Falcon Publications.

Aleister Crowley

Paederasty" and "With Dog and Dame," oblivious to the cautionary tale underlying the risqué subject matter: The book's protagonist finds the thrill of his mild erotic quirks waning over time, driving him to more extreme vices which ultimately culminates in madness and murder. At its core, the book is a critique of hedonism.

Despite the moral of *White Stains*, Crowley wrestled with his own young adult drives. Long periods of abstinence–

proscribed for magicians by medieval grimoires–proved counter-productive. While abstaining, sexual urges didn't dissipate, they consumed him. Rather than slowly starve the impulse to death, Crowley concluded a better strategy was simply to appease it and get on with the Great Work. He considered sex an impulse like thirst or hunger, best divorced from the emotional baggage which society attached to it. Later he would remark, "The stupidity of having had to waste uncounted priceless hours in chasing what ought to have been brought to the back door every evening with the milk![1] Alas, these countless priceless hours gained him a reputation whose repercussions he would suffer repeatedly throughout his lifetime: In 1900, on the basis of his character, he was barred from further advancement in the Hermetic Order of the Golden Dawn. Thus purposive indulgence collided with prudishness, and its eidolon was Queen Victoria.

Despite a childhood aversion to England's monarch, he admitted that "I was brought up in the faith that Queen Victoria would never die."[2] She symbolized the spirit of the age, where respectability and propriety was imposed on all expressions, both public and private. Social stagnation, Crowely believed, was rooted in this hypocritical and risible hyper-morality. It was in this context that Crowley and his climbing colleague, Oscar Eckenstien, "broke into shouts of joy and an impromptu war dance"[3] upon learning of Queen Victoria's death in 1901. By the time he wrote *The World's Tragedy* in February of 1909, his disdain had crystallized:

---

[1] Crowley, Aleister. *Confessions of Aleister Crowley*. London: Hill & Wang, 1969, p. 113.
[2] Chapter LXXVII. Work Worth While: Why? *Magick Without Tears*, See also an identical remark in *Confessions*, p. 41.
[3] *Confessions*, p. 216.

Priests who are celibates–outside of choir!
Maidens who rave in Lesbian desire:
The buck of sixty, cunning as a trapper,
Stalking the pig-tailed, masturbating flapper;
The creeping Jesus–Caution! We must shock it!–
With one hand through his turn-out breeches pocket;
Flagellants shrieking in our streets and schools,
Our men all hogs, and all our women ghouls:–
This is our England, pious dame and prude,
Who calls me blasphemous, unchaste, and rude![1]

By the end of 1909, Crowley began to realize the magical potential of sex. He was in Africa with his student Victor Neuburg, conducting a series of visionary experiments which would become *The Vision and the Voice*. While attempting to skry into the 14th of the 30 Enochian Aethyrs, Crowley found his progress blocked. Seized with inspiration, the magicians built a makeshift altar to the Greek god Pan and consecrated it with a sex act. Although Crowley was promiscuous, Neuburg was only his second male lover. The first, from his college days, left him with feelings of sin and guilt. This time, the homosexual encounter–in the open air under the desert sun, to the service of the Great Work– profoundly impacted him. He felt his ego–the Aleister Crowley raised in Victorian England by Plymouth Brethren parents–dissolve. In the language of initiation, he had crossed the Abyss.

Thus his attitude toward sex progressed significantly in the decade between entering college and writing *The Vision and the Voice*.[2] In his original view, the reproductive impulse was a distraction from spiritual work, and was best

---

[1] Crowley, Aleister. *The World's Tragedy*. Paris: privately printed, 1910, p. XXXVII; 2nd ed. Phoenix: New Falcon Publications, 1992.

[2] Crowley, Aleister. Liber LX: The Ab-ul-Diz Working. *The Vision and the Voice with Commentary and Other Papers*. York Beach: Weiser, 1998, p. 287-337.

sated to maximize the amount of time the mind could devote to higher goals. By 1909, he realized that the socially constructed boundaries called morality could literally block spiritual growth. By breaching taboos, Crowley realized he could break down these barriers, countermanding his social programming. This is what a later generation of rebels and devils would call "undoing yourself."[1]

Crowley's 1912 meeting with Theodor Reuss, head of the Ordo Templi Orientis, forged the last link in this chain of thought. In this legendary encounter, Reuss accused Crowley of revealing the O.T.O's central secret in *The Book of Lies*. When Crowley claimed innocence, Reuss directed him to Chapter 36, "*The Star Sapphire*." Reading the words, "Let the Adept be armed with his Magick Rood [and provided with his Mystic Rose]" with the understanding that Reuss interpreted these words as sexual symbols, the light bulb lit. The chain was completed. Sex was not merely a distraction from the Great Work, nor merely a barrier to advancement. It was the very vehicle of a potent form of magick which replaced the traditional claptrap with our own bodies.

To be fair, Crowley was already heading in this direction, as documented in the Abuldiz working, The *Scented Garden*, and *Liber Stellae Rubeae*.[2] But the Reuss encounter gathered those thoughts into coherent form. From this point, Crowley vigorously engaged not only in ritual sex[3] but other taboo experiences, all in the pursuit of spiritual insight.

---

[1] Hyatt, Christopher S. *Undoing Yourself with Energized Meditation and Other Devices*. 6th printing. Tempe, AZ; New Falcon Publications, 1993.
——— *Undoing Yourself Too*. Tempe, AZ; New Falcon Publications, 1998.

[2] *The Scented Garden of Abdullah the Satirist of Shiraz*, (Bagh-i-muattar). London, 1910:rpt Chicago: Teitan Press, 1991.
——— Liber Stellae Rubeae sub figura LXVI. *The Equinox I*, (7). 1912, p. 29-36.

[3] Symonds, John, and Grant, Kenneth. (eds). *The Magical Record of the Beast 666*. Quebec: Next Step, 1972; rpt. London: Duckworth, 1983.

Thus, when he took up painting around 1917, he advertised for "Dwarfs, Hunchbacks, Tattooed Women, Harrison Fisher Girls, Freaks of All Sorts, Coloured Women only if exceptionally ugly or deformed, to pose for artist." When he founded his Abbey of Thelema in Cefalù, Italy, in 1920, he took a page from Paul Gaugin and made the walls his canvas. The result was *La Chambre des Cauchemas* (Chamber of Nightmares), whose murals bombarded viewers with an array of frightful, disturbing and sexually explicit images. Crowley told visitors:

> There, in the corner, are Lesbians as large as life. Why do you feel shocked and turn away: or perhaps overtly turn to look again? Because, though you may have thought of such things, you have been afraid to face them. Drag all such thoughts into the light...'Tis only your mind that feels any wrong... Freud endeavors to break down such complexes in order to put the subconscious mind into a bourgeois respectability. That is wrong–the complexes should be broken down to give the sub-conscious will a chance to express itself freely..."[1]

Karl Germer, visiting the Abbey in 1926, confirmed the cathartic intent of these murals. "Beast evidently did all that as a medicine...against the English disease *par excellance*."[2]

Having fleshed out his psychological theory of magick, he began explaining it to his students. As Frank Bennett recounts his visit to Cefalù,

---

[1] Captain J.H.E. Townsend to J.F.C. Fuller, 19 April 1921, Harry Ransom Humanities Research Center, University of Texas at Austin.
[2] Karl Germer to Norman Mudd, 4 February 1926, Binder New 116, Yorke Collection, Warburg Institute, University of London.

[H]e began to talk about initiation, and said it was a matter of getting the sub-conscious mind at work, that when this subconscious mind was allowed to have full sway, without interference with the physical mind, illumination began for he said this subconscious mind was our Holy Guardian. He illustrated this by saying that everything was felt in this mind, and it is constantly urging its will upon the physical mind, and when these impressions, or inner desires, are restricted or suppressed, evil and all kind of trouble are the result.[1]

While Crowley disagreed with psychoanalysis,[2] this etiological theory or "evil and all kind of trouble" paraphrases Freud's ideas regarding repression, sublimation and neurosis.

He also experimented with drugs at this time, making them accessible to the Abbey's visitors to rob them of their mystique and allure. His view on drug addiction paralleled *White Stains'* warning about sex, and, by extension, apply to all behaviors driven by the pleasure principle: Anything pursued hedonistically ultimately leads to moral collapse; but placing it in service to the Will protects the magician from addiction or other apostasies.[3] This calls to mind *The Book of*

---

[1] Frank Bennett. (1921). Magical Record of Frater Progradior in a Retirement at. Cefalu Sicily. Yorke Collection.

[2] Crowley, Aleister. An improvement upon psychoanalysis. *Vanity Fair*, December 1916, p. 60, 137; rpt. Hymenaeus Beta and Richard Kaczynski (eds.)., *The Revival of Magick and Other Essays*. Tempe, AZ: New Falcon, 1998.

[3] Crowley, Aleister. *The Diary of a Drug Fiend*. London: W. Collins & Co., 1922.

――― The great drug delusion. A New York Specialist (pseud.) *The English Review*, July 1922, p. 65-70.

――― The drug panic. A London Physician (pseud). *The English Review*, (7). 1912, p. 29-36.

――― Crowley found these principles harder than expected to put into practice in *Liber Tzaba vel Nike (The Fountain of Hyacinth)*, Binder A4-A5, Yorke Collection.

the Law's instruction, "To worship me take wine and strange drugs whereof I will tell my prophet, & he be drunk thereof! They shall not harm ye at all." (*AL* ii.22). On this passage, Crowley cautioned:

> Lest there be folly, let me say that this passage does not license reckless debauch. The use of drugs and drink is to be strictly and act of Magick. Compare what is said in the First Chapter with regard to the use of the functions of sex.[1]

Thus he reiterated that explorations of the human psyche's dark underbelly be intentional and purposive.

Other experiments at Cefalù involved gender bending, the *menage a trois*, sado-masochism and coprophagia. While Crowley considered this legitimate psychological research, he realized the controversial nature of his work. Between the publication of *The Diary of a Drug Fiend* and the unfortunate death from typhoid of an Abbey visitor, the tabloids of the time unleased an astonishing series of attacks. Crowley's reaction:

> I regard all these people, all England with rare individual exceptions, as moral cowards with all that that implies. Sir Richard Burton had an experience precisely similar to mine. So had Christopher Columbus. So had Darwin. Their instinctive dread of a man who dares the unknown. *Omne Ignotum pro terribili* and such a man may bring it to their door at any moment. The whole history of science illustrates this. Science is now tolerated because Science has been at pains to prove that (on the balance) it has benefited mankind. I, bringing as I do, new knowledge of the unknown, and obviously the mark of fear, horror and persecution.[2]

---

[1] Crowley, Aleister. Duplicate typescript with mss corrections of part of the unpublished commentary on the 'Book of the Law,' Oasis of Nefta, Al-Djerid, Tunisia, 1923. Rare Books Department, Z. Smith Reynolds Library, Wake Forest University, Winston-Salem, N.C.

[2] Aleister Crowley to Norman Mudd, 20 April 1924, Yorke Collection.

Small wonder that Crowley's records from Cefalù were seized and destroyed by H.M. Customs as pornographic when he tried returning them to England.

In the end, Crowley became the eidolon or reflection of those impulses denied by society which Queen Victoria symbolized. Confronting the Beast meant confronting those repressed impulses, with the resulting ordeal dubbed "The Vision of the Demon Crowley." Indeed, those who persevered and saw through the smoke screen became his staunchest advocates–Gerald Yorke, Louis Wilkinson, Karl Germer and Israel Regardie among them–while those who bolted off were convinced they had narrowly escaped the clutches of the devil. "The main danger seems to be getting caught on the reef of his own interpretation," Kenneth Grant commented. "But this, after all, is but the proper function of the 'Demon Crowley'!"[1] Likewise, when Crowley began a campaign to rehabilitate his reputation, Gerald Yorke neatly summarized the function of the Great Beast:

> To my mind, part of your 'mission,' if I may use a word I mistrust, is to show that the code of morals of what a Thelemite calls the Old Aeon has been superseded, and that now any act is right provided it is done in the right way, as in interpretation of True Will. It must have been your Will to be the Beast, and a whitewashed Beast is an useless commercial article.[2]

Crowley must have been convinced, for he continued living the rest of his life with no apologies.

---

[1] Kenneth Grant, private communication, 5 December 1989.
[2] Gerald Yorke to Aleister Crowley, 20 March 1928, Binder New 116, Yorke Collection.

Aleister Crowley
Also known as
*The Beast 666, The Wickedest Man Alive
and The Prophet of the New Aeon*

Analogues in Other Traditions

The notion of sacrifice–literally to make sacred, or to find the holy in the mundane–is not unique to Crowley.

Hasidic Jews find God through the "enjoyable and necessary acts of ordinary life."[1] Early forms of Hasidism's *Chabad* mysticism included practices like *Haalat ha-Nitzotzot* ("elevating the sparks," or recognizing everything as a manifestation of God), *'Avodah he-Hipukh* ("worship through inversion," where self-fulfillment comes from joining things–even God–with its opposite), and its extension *Yeridah Le-Tsorekh 'Aliyah* ("descent for the purpose of ascent"). When the *Tzaddikim* began discussing things like

---

[1] Cantor, Norman F. The Sacred Chain: The History of the Jews. New York: Schocken, 1988.

the sanctity of sin, exploring the *Sitra Ahra* (the "opposite tree" or *Qlippoth*), or discussing how one can find God by exploring the desire to kill one's neighbor, these practices were eliminated as dangerous.[1]

In Tantra, followers of the *Kaula* branch and *vama marg* or "left hand path" advocate the well-known *panchamakaras* or *panchatattva* ritual. Literally meaning "five elements," it involves partaking five substances which are usually religiously prohibited. The five items, in Sanskrit, all begin with the letter M; hence, this ritual is often referred to as "the five M's." The items are *madya* or *madir*–(wine or liquor), *matsya* (fish), *m–msa* (meat), *mudr*–(parched grain) and *maithun*–(sex, often out of caste). The concept behind this ritual is that which drove Crowley's explorations: Social taboos, broken in a religious context, can produce great spiritual advancement.[2]

Finally the masters known as the Aghori represent such an extreme manifestation of this formula that they are the object of fear and awe in India, believed to have transcended all boundaries of good and evil. Their best-known activities center around mankind's greatest taboo, death. *Aghori* will sleep in cemeteries, often sharing the same coffin with

---

[1] Ariel, David S. *The Mystic Quest: An Introduction to Jewish Mysticism.* New York: Schocken, 1988. Elior, Rachel. *The Paradoxical Ascent to God: The Kabbalistic Theosophy of Habad Hasidism.* New York: State University of New York Press, 1993.

[2] Garrison, Omar. Tantra: *The Yoga of Sex. New York*: Causeway, 1964. Geuerstwin, Georg. *Tantra: The Path of Ecstasy.* Boston: Shambhala, 1998. Douglas, Nik, and Slinger, Penny. *Sexual Secrets: The Alchemy of Ecstasy.* New York: Destiny, 1979; rpt. New York: Inner Traditions.

corpses. They observe and wait, ready to celebrate the popping of the body's skullcap, for to them that represents the final release of the soul. Once or twice in a lifetime, an *Aghori* will consume a piece of human brain, the first place to show the stirring of the spirit and the last place from which it is vacated. Even necrophilia is not unknown.[1] By immersing themselves in the most dreaded of all things–human death and decay–the *Aghorii* seek not only to come to terms with death, but also–like Crowley, the *Chabad* mystics and the *Tantrikas*–to come a little closer to understanding God.

---

[1] Svoboda, Robert E. *Aghora: At the Left Hand of God.* Brotherhood of Life: Albuquerque, NM, 1986.

DR. ISRAEL REGARDIE

Ceremonial Magic
an introductory guide, by an eminent modern
occultist, to the mechanisms of ceremonial magic,
based on the rituals of the Golden Dawn.

BASIC PRINCIPLES OF MAGIC

Chapter 1 from **Ceremonial Magic**
A Guide To The Mechanisms of Ritual
New Falcon Publications, Eleventh Printing 2022

Dr. Israel Regardie

It may be asked for what purpose this book has been written. Why should one bother with ceremonial magic of this type? The question is valid. But in view of the fact that so much has been written in recent years about magic itself, the answer should be so clearly apparent to any student of the subject that I do not feel disposed to cope with it here and now at any length.

One may mention first of all *The Mystical Qalabah* of Dion Fortune, which provides the theoretical basis of ritual magic. Then there are the several books of W. E. Butler, all on the same topic, excellent texts for the student to study for a long time. William Gray's *Ladder of Lights* is a masterpiece to be put in a similar category with the book by Dion Fortune mentioned above. Gareth Knight has written a fine little book *The Practice of Ritual Magic*. Certainly the writings of Aleister Crowley on this topic must never be neglected; he is the primary expositor on this subject in modern times. *Gems From the Equinox* as well as his *Magick in Theory and Practice* will give the student a good deal of material which may take years to assimilate and to use properly.

A couple of my own books may be consulted to considerable advantage. *The Golden Dawn* is a *must*; I can say this without any sense of egotism for I was only the editor, not the author of the material contained in those (original) four volumes. *The Tree of Life* may help to clarify and coordinate a great deal of the apparently disconnected material of both Crowley and The Golden Dawn. Finally, *Foundations of Practical Magic* (Aquarian Press, 1979) should be mentioned as a general introduction to the whole practical side of the subject. With this material assimilated, what follows in this book should not be too mysterious, nor the motives for practising it.

What is to be gained from the frequent, or, even better, the daily psycho-spiritual sensitivity. The student who has spent some time on the basic disciplines described in *Twelve Steps to Spiritual Enlightenment*, or some other similar regimen, will find himself in a position to obtain a very great deal more from the ritual than the student approaching this without due preparation.

Despite the fact that illumination is in effect, a sudden and immediate event, it is nonetheless equally true that enhancing the sensitivity of the organism may well prepare the way for such an event to occur. There are no absolute rules laid down anywhere that guarantee enlightenment. 'The spirit bloweth where it listeth.' No man is in a position to say who, or when, or why any one individual is subject to this descent of the holy spirit.

The fact remains, however, that most systems of initiation are predicated on preparing the organism for this most precious experience. There is to be a refining of the elemental vehicles through which the Self may function, an equilibration of the total organism so that when enlightenment does occur, the stresses and strains to which the organism may be subject will not disrupt its natural and integrated functions. Insanity is not one of the goals of spiritual growth and development–although it occurs far too often to make one feel comfortable when contemplating the present occult scene. Proper preparation, self-discipline and daily practice are still the time-honoured approaches to the gateway of the higher mysteries and character-transformation.

One of the more effective traditional methods of preparing a room for use as a temple for active ritual work or for quiet meditation, is called "Opening by Watch Tower". It may seem to the beginner frightfully complex and difficult. In reality, however, the beginner frightfully complex and difficult. In reality, however, when studied, and above all when practised, it becomes remarkably simple and direct. Besides possessing its own utility as well as charm, the method is capable of development in a variety of different directions so that, if need be, it can be elaborated into a major ritual for all occasions and all purposes. It may require some study first, followed by some little practical experience over a period of weeks or months–depending on personal ability, as well as time available–before this conclusion may be recognized.

It incorporates most of the better features that once characterized the Golden Dawn. These include the Pentagram and Hexagram Rituals, which need to be studied and meditated upon. In a special sense, the Pentagram is another ritual which, with deliberation, can become a armamentarium of approaches which the casual student may not perceive at first sight.

The term 'Watch-Towers' is borrowed from the Enochian system of Dr. John Dee and Edward Kelley. They theorized that at each quarter of the earth stood a tower guarded by angelic and elemental forces. These metaphysical concepts are represented in actual practice by the Elemental Tablets placed at the four points of the compass in the temple or room being used.

The full comprehension of these Tablets demands close attention to and study of the Enochian Section of Vol. IV of *The Golden Dawn*. Admittedly, to draw and paint the Tablets requires the expenditure of much time and energy, and this might make some students hesitate before going any further. However, a compromise is available, lessening the demand for time and energy. The sigils at the top of each Tablet or Watchtower may be painted on board–or any other material the student desires to use–having the arbitrary dimensions of about six inches by six inches.

These sigils from *The Golden Dawn*, which gives the colours, etc., to be used in their construction, are reproduced in Vol. IV of *The Golden Dawn*. Pastels or crayons or coloured paper may be used. If one has skill enough, oil or acrylic paints may be used, but these can be messy unless the student has previously acquired experience with them. I am partial to the use of poster colours on Bristol board, spraying them with clear lacquer a day or so after they have achieved full drying. These should be hung or pinned on the wall in the appropriate quarter.

I do not suggest that the student plunges headlong into the working of this ritual. There need be no hurry. What is required is some familiarization with the content of the ritual so that the ongoing movement may be perceived. Then a few trial runs, as it were, may be attempted just to get the feel. With these trials runs, some of the ritual wording may be memorized. This should not provide much difficulty. I suggest working with the written text in front of one for some little time, in which case memorization will occur by rote and without strain or effort.

This book is divided into sections showing how the ritual is built up from scratch. There is also an Appendix which gives the Pentagram and Hexagram Rituals and other pertinent material. These should be memorized so that full attention can be given thereafter to the Watchtower Ritual itself. This is another reason why the student should not hasten to arrive at the end immediately.

Incidentally, I am using the word 'student' throughout. We are all students, and should be forever. There is so much to learn and apply. Words such as 'magus', or 'adeptus minor', or other such grandiloquent titles, have been deliberately omitted in favour of this simple word 'student'. All of us are in this one simple category.

The ritual itself is first presented in all its simplicity. Study it well. Then in a succeeding section, additions will be made. These additions are extrapolated from the elemental Grades of the Order of the Golden Dawn and from Vol. I, No. 8 *Equinox*. Note them well, please. In these grades, the officiating officer invokes the Elements by a specific process so that they may influence the aura and character of the candidate undergoing initiation. This specific process is added in the appropriate place to the Watchtower Ritual, lengthening it a little bit, but rendering it not only more explicit to the student, but more potent. It would not be amiss, then, to read into this statement that the Watchtower Ritual may be turned into a ritual of self-initiation.

I would like to remind the reader that this study has made no mention deliberately of some of the basic psycho-spiritual techniques operative in ceremonial magic. The assumption of the God-forms at the appropriate quarters, the method of vibration of divine and angelic names, and the use of spirit-vision are some of the major methods to be used with a rubic of this kind. I have omitted them, however, in order to keep this study as simple as possible. When the student becomes more adept in using this form of ritual, he may gradually add to his armamentarium these other devices which are fully described in other textbooks, notably *The Middle Pillar*. Though this book is now considerably outdated and will be rewritten in the near future, it is still a useful book of instruction.

One of the reasons for starting off the ceremony with the Pentagram Ritual is not only a clear a space for the working, but to insure that the entire operation is under the aegis of the Higher Self. This is one of the major characteristics of the Golden Dawn outlook. In one of the higher grades, a clause in the Oath is to the effect that in each operation of magic the student pledges to work under and to employ only the highest divine names that he knows. 'For by names and images are all powers awakened and reawakened.'

A later section then reproduces the Prayers of the Elements that are given at the close of each of the elemental grades. These are long beautiful prayers expressing the aspirations and nature of each elemental kingdom. Each prayer may be used *in toto* in the appropriate place; these will be clearly indicated. They are long, it is true, but they impart much beauty and power to the ritual. If too long for the average student, they may well be abbreviated.

For many months, in the mid-thirties, I used a variation of this ritual with about a half-dozen sentences extrapolated from each prayer. They picked up the essence of the longer prayer and served my purpose very well. Each student might attempt this on his own behalf if he finds using each prayer lengthens the ritual too much.

Finally, there is another section which uses one of the Golden Dawn invocations from the 5=6 Ritual, together with the closing paragraph of the so-called Bornless Ritual. Contrary to some recently expressed opinions, this was *never* an official ritual of the Order. Not that it matters very much. It has a quality of its own, adding a species of fervour and intensity to the ritual which converts it into an Invocation of the Higher Self, or the Holy Guardian Angel, so-called.

Crowley, at various periods of his life, seemed forever unable to decide whether the Holy Guardian Angel or the Higher and Divine Genius of The Golden Dawn was the same as the Higher Self, or an Angelic being totally independent of man. The bulk of his writing however tends to identify them–the Higher Self *is* the Holy Guardian Angel. This is more or less confirmed, if we need confirmation, by Blavatsky's remarks in *The Secret Doctrine* that 'The Watcher, or the divine prototype, is at the upper rung of the ladder of being; the shadow at the lower. Withal, the *Monad* of every living being…*is an individual Dhyan Chohan (god), distinct from others, a kind of spiritual individuality of its own, during one special Manvantara.*' This is further confirmed by Mathers in his profound essay 'On Man, the Microcosm' in Vol. I of *The Golden Dawn* in which he relates the Higher Self to the Divine Genius as an Angel, part of an ever-ascending hierarchy of spiritual beings.

> The Shining Flame of the Divine Fire, the *Kether* of the Body, is the Real Self of the Incarnation…This *Yechidah* is the only part of the man which can truly say – EHEIEH, I am. This is then but the Kether of the Assiah of the Microcosm, that is, it is the highest part of man as Man…Behind *Yechidah* are Angelic and Archangelic Forces of which *Yechidah* is the manifestor. It is therefore the Lower Genius or Viceroy of the Higher Genius which is beyond, an Angel Mighty and Terrible. This Great Angel is the higher Genius, beyond which are the Archangelic and Divine.

This, in effect, completes the study of the ritual, beginning with its use as simply a means of preparing a room for use as a temple and winding up with an invocation of the Higher Self.

One writer recently ridiculed me indirectly by deriding the idea that in working a ritual good 'head of steam' has to be generated. I would like to remind him, and others of the same ilk, that an example of good ritual, from a technical point of view, is to be found in the Masonic Order. I doubt if there is to found anywhere else in the world comparable accoutrements, environment, training, etc. They are very impressive to watch. Any Mason will confirm this–without betraying any of the secrets he is bound to withhold from the non-Mason. In my teens I was a member of the Order of De Molay, a junior Masonic organization, started by Masons, superintended by Masons, and in effect, conducted by Masons. It had the same beautiful paraphernalia, the same superb coaching to produce the right sage effect, the same kind of pomp, order and stateliness. In a word, its rituals are copies of Masonic rituals without the traditional Masonic mystery. If this is my critic's idea of good magical ritual, I can only assure him that he is way off. They are stately and very impressive, without doubt, but they are far from magical, no matter how well the officiants have learned their lines nor how smoothly or effectively the team may operate. Nothing is achieved on a magical level.

Working correctly with ritual has to evoke a species of inner excitation, more than merely a mood, which exalts the mind to reach upwards to its own divine root. A cold, stately perfectly executed rite will never achieve this, no matter how clear and accurate the visualizations, etc., may be.

A few words are necessary about equipment and paraphernalia. These are matters to which the beginner usually bestows undue attention, using them unconsciously as devices to deter him from beginning any magical work whatsoever. It seems too appallingly difficult to get everything together–a room with privacy, the symbols upon the altar, and the so-called elemental weapons. When reading the instructions preceding magical rituals, there seem to be so many requisites that are practically beyond him at this stage of development as to cause him to lose heart and interest.

I would like to insist that so many of these can be simplified down to the point where even the novice can comply without complicating his life and his intellectual capabilities to any major degree. For example: the altar can be almost any small table about waist-high. Spread on it a black cloth–black, because it is neutral; some other colour would attract one's attention unnecessarily. The basic symbols to be placed on it are those of the Golden Dawn–the red cross and the white triangle. Surely it is not difficult to cut from white pasteboard a white equilateral triangle with a base of two or three inches?

The cross does not necessarily carry with it a Christian significance. In Volume I of *The Golden Dawn*, the knowledge lectures ascribe different meaning to the several forms of the cross. For our purpose here, however, it is the equal-armed cross that is used and represents equilibrium and a balanced disposition of whatever elements are involved.

The cross should be equal-armed (actually comprised of five squares) about three inches high or wide and painted red. The cross should be placed above the white triangle, towards the middle of the altar. Now that is not very difficult, is it?

So far as the instruments are concerned: if you have made them, well and good. Full instructions have been given in *The Golden Dawn* that are not too difficult to comply with. The Watchtower Ritual actually will comprise a sort of consecration ceremony if you have made them. If not, it does not matter. At the East, on the altar, place a small fan made from a sheet of typing paper that you have carefully folded, as any child will show you, to represent the element of Air. In the South, for the element of Fire, use an incense stick; or if you do not have any, just place a small unused book of matches in the right place. In the West, to represent Water, a small glass of water. While in the North, a few crumbs of bread and a few grains of salt may be placed on a tiny saucer or platter to represent Earth. It is just as simple as that. For the element of Spirit, place a freshly cut flower, a rose or whatever else is in season, on top of the triangle and cross in the centre of the altar. This completely solves the whole complex problem of instruments and so forth.

Robes, special clothing, collars, breast-plates and lamens, all of these considerations may be left alone until such time as the student feels ready to undertake their manufacture and use. Washing or bathing before the ceremony may be enough at the outset. After he has studied the subject sufficiently intensively from the textbooks where these topics are dealt with, then he may feel sufficiently secure to attempt their use. On the other hand, if he fares well in the ceremony, he may feel no need to complicate matters by the use of technical paraphernalia and equipment.

When the proper time arrives for coping with such details, the books already mentioned will provide the necessary information. However, Robert Wang has recently compiled a book based on *The Golden Dawn* and some verbal information from me that should fill the bill even better. It is entitled *The Secret Temple* (Samuel Weiser, 1980). It takes the basic Golden Dawn material and expands it from the point of view of the practically-minded student who wants to equip his temple properly and by his own efforts. Full and detailed instruction is given on the manufacture of the elemental and other weapons, banners of the East and West, Pillars of the Temple, the altar, robes, and many other similar matters.

But again, let me insist, leave all of this detail severely alone until you have acquired some expertise with ceremonial work, and feel the need for more adequate and complete material to work with.

It would be ideal if you had a room which you could reserve only for meditation and magical working. Today, however, with more people living in apartments than ever before, and space being so very limited, this may be impossible. If it is impossible, use whatever room is available–the bedroom, the living room, the den, or whatever. You should be assured of temporary privacy; that at least is an essential, so have a lock or bolt on this door. Or request those you live with not to enter your room at certain hours when you are working.

All problems relating to the mere technician of ritual procedure should be solved in the same way, simply and easily and directly. This is why some preliminary study and meditation is required, so that you know what you are doing and why. Do not do things blindly, merely because a book tells you to. Understand the reasons for what you do and what you employ. They are basically simple and the existing literature, in spite of some complicating features, really does explain the fundaments. Mystification has no part in magic. Simplicity and sincerity and enthusiasm have.

James Wasserman

Lord, I thank You for my creation
I acknowledge that I am a star
Whose orbit and purpose I am
pledged to follow and pursue
Free me from bondage of false selves
That I may know and do my True Will
To the glory of Thine Ineffable Name

AUMGN

PULLING LIBERTY'S TEETH

James Wasserman

"A well regulated Militia, being necessary to the security of a free State, the right of the people to keep and bear Arms, shall not be infringed."
                    -Second Amendment to the U.S. Constitution

"Those who beat their swords into plowshares will do the plowing for those who didn't."
                    -Self-Evident Fact of Life

A "MILLION" MISINFORMED MOMS

To paraphrase a famous gun-controller of old, May 14, 2000 is "a date which will live in infamy." A group consisting mostly of women and estimated at between 150,000 and 500,000, forewent the traditional family pleasures associated with the annual Mother's Day holiday to rally around TV personality and former Kmart spokeswoman Rosie O'Donnell. She was accompanied by such well-known gun confiscation luminaries as Diane Feinstein, Maxine Waters and Sarah Brady, all of whom spent the day expressing their contempt for the aspirations of America's founders, and their disdain for law-abiding Americans who believe in the Second Amendment. It was the first time in this writer's memory that a mass protest was aimed directly at the Bill of Rights.

Many of the "Moms" at the march were undoubtedly veterans of the Anti-War movement of the 1960s and 70s, when the youthful idealism of a generation was masterfully manipulated by the anti-American Left. Now in middle-age, those who never woke up to the assault on Liberty embodied by the Nanny State, bared their teeth for a direct attack against the hated "rich, white, slave-owning men" who built the greatest, most prosperous, and freest nation in the history of the world. Professor Camille Paglia describes the march as "... the gun control protest organized (as the major media is finally admitting) by the sister-in-law of Hillary Clinton's longtime lawyer pal and hatchet woman, surly Susan Thomases..."[1] Surprised?

THE SECOND AMENDMENT: AN INDIVIDUAL RIGHT?

The "shot heard round the world" was fired during the first battle of the American Revolution on April 19, 1775 at British soldiers seeking to enforce British gun control laws by confiscating weapons and gunpowder belonging to the citizens of Concord, Massachusetts. Both Dr. Joyce Lee Malcolm in *To Keep and Bear Arms* and Dr. Stephen P. Halbrook in *That Every Man Be Armed* have provided prodigious, compelling and common sense scholarship to prove that the Second Amendment is a right possessed by the people[2]. If the reader has any doubt of this, he or she is referred to these two scholars. On the other hand, the text of the amendment itself, especially its phrase "the right of the people" may be considered indicative. See also similar use of the phrase "the people" in First, Fourth, Ninth and Tenth Amendments.

---

[1] Paglia, Camile. "The Million Mom March: What a Crock!" Salon.com, 17 May 2000.
[2] Malcom, Joyce Lee. *To Keep and Bear Arms*. Harvard University Press, 1994. Halbrook, Stephen. *That Every Man be Armed*. The Independent Institute, 1994.

The passionate and brilliant writings and speeches collected in *The Federalist Papers*, *The Anti-Federalist Papers* and *The Debate on the Constitution*, establish beyond a shadow of a doubt that the right of the individual American to keep and bear arms was one of the most important guarantees brought forth in favor of the plan to consolidate the American Republic.[3] At least eight of the original thirteen states had provisions in their constitutions that included recognition of the right of private citizens to keep and bear arms. The words of the early leaders of America eloquently expressed their view that an armed populace is: 1) a natural check against tyranny, 2) the first line of defense against enemy attack, and 3) a natural force for the right ordering of society. The founders well understood the liberties acknowledged by the Bill of Rights could only be held by a citizenry willing and able to protect its freedom, by force if necessary, from those who would attempt to seize it. The Second Amendment is Liberty's Teeth.

TYRANNY: MERELY AN ANTIQUATED EIGHTEENTH CENTURY CONCERN?

In 1787 Noah Webster wrote,

> Before a standing army can rule, the people must be disarmed; as they are in almost every kingdom of Europe. The supreme power in America cannot enforce unjust laws by the sword; because the whole body of the people are armed, and constitute a force superior to any bands of regular troops that can be, on any pretense, raised in the United States.[4]

---

[3] See *The Federalist Papers*, edited by Clinton Rossiter, Penguin Books, *The Anti-Federalist Papers* and the *Constitutional Convention Debates*, edited by Ralph Ketcham, Penguin Books, and *The Debate on the Constitution*, (two volumes) edited by Bernard Bailyn, The Library of America.
[4] *A Citizen of America*, Philadelphia October 17, 1787, quoted in *The Debate on the Constitution*, Part 1, p. 155.

When Bill Clinton was sworn into office for his first term, he warmly remembered his former professor at Georgetown University, Carroll Quigley. Aside from being the recipient of such a singular honor, Quigley may have helped shape some of the attitudes toward the Second Amendment held by the most anti-gun president in American history. Quigley wrote in his 1966 tome *Tragedy and Hope*,

> In a period of specialist weapons the minority who have such weapons can usually force the majority who lack them to obey; thus a period of specialist weapons tends to give rise to a period of minority rule and authoritarian government. But a period of amateur weapons is a period in which all men are roughly equal in military power, a majority can compel a minority to yield, and majority rule or even democratic government tends to rise...[6]

At the present time, there seems to be little reason to doubt that the specialist weapons of today will continue to dominate the military picture into the foreseeable future. If so, there is little reason to doubt that authoritarian rather than democratic political regimes will dominate the world into the same foreseeable future.[7]

Undeterred by this nightmarish conclusion, Quigley quickly displays the confidence in alternate solutions and concern for the "quality of life" that undoubtedly touched the heart of his young protege;

A period that is not democratic in its political structure is not necessarily bad, and may well be one in which people can live a rich and full social or intellectual life whose value may be even more significant than a democratic political or military structure.[8]

---

[6] Quigley, Carroll. *Tragedy and Hope*. Macmillan, 1966, p. 34.
[7] *Ibid.*, pp. 1200-1201.
[8] *Ibid.*, p. 1201.

OVERTURNING THE CONSTITUTION

The civilian disarmament movement is working relentlessly to avoid the one legal means of enacting gun control-namely to amend the Constitution to either repeal the Second Amendment or to legally modify it. No lovers of the limitations on government imposed by the Constitution, gun control zealots are well aware of the obstacles placed in the path of "reformers" who seek to change it. A two-thirds majority of Congress may propose amendments which must then be adopted by three-fourths of the states. Even with these protections, such idiotic amendments as Prohibition will occur. However, this is not the concern of the civilian disarmament crowd who seek to bypass the Constitution altogether.

As Jaime Sneider wrote,

> [T]he language of organizers and supporters of the Million Mom March hints at a growing trend that culminated in yesterday's March. The (generally left-leaning) disgruntled individuals who have failed politically in getting gun control measures passed have come to support Constitutional Nullification... Perhaps the scariest thing about the gun control movement is that they want to blur the existence of truth itself. According to their own words, gun-control leaders will not stop until the private ownership of guns is illegal and the Constitution overthrown. As such, they encourage nullification of the universal moral truths contained within that document. As the gun control activists pursue their agenda by any means necessary, supporting ever larger and more intrusive government, the true ethical purpose of the Second Amendment will only become more apparent.[9]

---

9 Sneider, Jaime. "Taking Aim at the Constitution:' Columbia Daily Spectator as reported by National Review, 15 May 2000.

REASONS FOR REBELLION

The following news report is especially instructive in that regard.

> United Nations Secretary-General Kofi Annan has called on the international community to stem the proliferation of small arms across the world. He told a special meeting of the Security Council that restricting the flow of such weapons would be a key challenge in preventing conflict in the next century. Estimates of the number of firearms in the world range from 100 million to 500 million. Mr. Annan said there was 'no single tool of conflict so widespread, so easily available, and so difficult to restrict, as small arms' ... In his report Mr. Annan recommended that member states should: 'Adopt gun control laws including a prohibition of unrestricted trade and private ownership of small arms.'[10] [emphasis added]

---

[10] BBC Online News Network, 25 September 1999.

This is nothing less than an open call to overturn the U.S. Constitution and the Second Amendment in favor of "international law"–the infamous New World Order.

GUN CONTROL AND AMERICAN CULTURE

On the day of the march, an estimated 20,000 U.S. gun laws were on the books. To quote Ms. Paglia again,

> The Million Moms would do much more for this country if they would focus on the breakdown of family and community ties that produce sociopaths like the goons who shoot up schools and day care centers. It was parental irresponsibility and neglect, and not simply the availability of guns, that were ultimately at the root of the Columbine massacre, where home-barbecue propane tanks had been converted into bombs.

	Non-Gun Owners (Adolescent Grp.)	**Illegal Gun Owners**	**Legal Gun Owners**
Street Crimes	24%	74%	14%
Gun Crimes	1%	24%	0%

The Moms might also have consulted the 1994 report of the rabidly anti-gun Janet Reno-led Justice Department, *Urban Delinquency and Substance Abuse: Initial Findings Research Summary*[11] (see Table). Boys who own legal firearms were found to have the lowest rate of compared to both those owning illegal guns, and those owning none.

The study attributed the disparity in part to the "socialization into gun ownership," of boys with their fathers who owned guns for hunting and sport. One might suppose the close parental bonding would be equally salutary for young girl shooters as well.

---

[11] Discussed by Robert W. Lee in *The New American*, 24, April 2000.

CREATING PUBLIC OPINION

The American public is fed a daily dose of cooked statistics reminiscent of George Orwell's novel 1984. However, the tragic consequences of this propaganda on national policy threaten real life and real people. The general willingness of the American population to believe the lies of politicians and media spin-masters, and the lack of interest in alternative news sources, are disturbing. An informed electorate can make decisions. A brainwashed mass merely regurgitates its conditioning.

Geoffrey Dickens, Senior Analyst of the respected Media Research Center, detailed his group's two-year study of the treatment of gun related issues by four evening news shows (ABC's World News Tonight, the CBS Evening News, CNN's The World Today, and NBC's Nightly News) and three morning broadcasts (ABC's Good Morning America, CBS's This Morning, and NBC's Today). The study tracked these shows from July 1, 1997 to June 30, 1999.[12]

The criteria for categorization of stories as either "anti-gun" or "pro-gun" were the following: anti-gun statements were defined as ideas like "violent crimes occur because of guns;" and "gun control prevents crime;" pro-gun statements included ideas such as "criminals, not guns, cause crime," "Americans have a constitutional right to keep and bear arms," and "Concealed carry laws help reduce crime." If such statements in a news reports were weighted in a ratio of 1.5:1, the story or segment was identified as either anti-gun or pro-gun. If the ratio was less than 1.5:1, the story was regarded as neutral.

---

[12] Dickens, Geoffrey. "Outgunned: How the Network News Media are Spinning the Gun Control Debate:' *The American Rifleman*, April 2000.

In 653 gun policy stories, the study found stories advocating more gun control outnumbered stories opposing gun control by 357 to 36–a ratio of nearly 10:1 (with 260 categorized as neutral). Anti-gun sound bites were twice as frequent as those with a pro-gun message, 412 to 209. Gun control advocates appeared on morning shows 82 times compared with 37 gun rights advocates and 58 neutral spokesmen. There were 300 evening news segments which rated as follows: 164 anti-gun, 20 pro-gun, and 116 neutral. Talking heads were gun control advocates by a 2:1 ratio. Of 353 gun policy segments on morning news shows, anti-gun stories outnumbered pro-gun by 193 to 15 or a ratio of 13:1 (with 145 categorized as neutral).

A FAMILIAR HALF-DOZEN ANTI-GUN LIES

1. The "Dead Children" Lie

In the words of David Kopel, "A full listing of the lies told by the antigun lobby could fill a book."[13] Perhaps the most egregious of such is the Myth of the Dead Children. How many days go by each week when some government hack or media news reader doesn't bow his or her head and solemnly intone the quantitative figures of children killed every day by guns. Our minds are forced to conjure images of more than a hundred children a week lying dead like little well-fed Biafrans in front of Daddy's bloody night stand.

In truth, the per-capita number of fatal gun accidents among children is at its lowest level since 1903, when statistics started being kept. Furthermore, the actual number of

---

[13] Kopel, David, Research Director of the Independence Institute. "An Army of Gun Lies:' *National Review*, 17 April 2000.

child firearm fatalities is also declining every year, even as the numbers of people with firearms in their homes increases. By way of example, in 1995, there were 1,400 accidental firearm deaths in America of which 30 involved children four and younger, while 170 involved the five- to fourteen-year-old age bracket (thus 200 children in total). By comparison 2,900 children died in motor vehicles, 950 died by drowning, and 1,000 died by fire and burns. *More children die in bicycle accidents each year than by firearms*[14]. Nobody wants even one child to die. Reducing firearm accidents even further is the goal of the NRA's brilliant Eddie Eagle Program, a common sense and effective firearm safety educational effort for children—which has been boycotted, ignored, and slandered by the gun banners.

The mournful statistical mantra of the mass media/ civilian disarmament lobby are cynically based on counting young adults as children. Thus a teenage gangland slaying, a young fleeing felon shot by a police officer, a jealous twenty-one year-old shooting his wife's seducer in a bar, or a crack deal gone bad, are all counted as "children who die by firearms." Accidents are a part of life and cannot be regulated away. But the shamelessness with which these statistics are manipulated to provide fodder for those seeking to expand the range of government control is important to note.

2. The "Guns Cause Crime" Lie

"Normal" people do not turn into crazed maniacs when a gun is placed in their hands any more than guns levitate from tables, pockets, or closets to discharge themselves and kill

---

[14] Lott, John Jr. *More Guns, Less Crime*. University of Chicago Press, 1998, p. 9.

innocent people. The oft-repeated statement that a gun in the home is 43 times more likely to kill a family member than a criminal is another purposeful distortion of the truth to serve a political agenda. "Of the 43 deaths, 37 are suicides; and while there are obviously many ways in which a person can commit suicide, only a gun allows a small woman a realistic opportunity to defend herself at a distance from a large male predator.[15] Another of the big lies of the gun control lobby is that most people are killed by people they know. This argument is concocted from the FBI Uniform Crime Report which states that family murders account for 18 percent of murders, while 40 percent were those who "knew" their victims. The category of "those who knew their victim" however includes drug dealers and buyers, prostitutes and clients, cab drivers killed by passengers, rival gang members involved in turf wars, and murderous barroom brawlers.

Perhaps a more telling statistic is that in 1988, more than 89 percent of adult murderers had adult criminal records.[16] To put it in even simpler terms-bad people do bad things.

John Lott's monumental study of gun ownership in the United States covered all 3,054 U.S. counties from 1977 to 1992, supplemented with data for 1993 and 1994. He reached the following conclusion, "Of all the methods studied so far by economists, the carrying of concealed handguns appears to be the most cost-effective method for reducing crime.[17] The positive effect of reducing violent crime is particularly

---

[15] Kopel, David, "*An Army of Gun Lies.*" *National Review*, 17 April 2000.

[16] Lott, John Jr. *More Guns, Less Crime.* University of Chicago Press, 1988.

[17] *Ibid.*, p. 20.

significant for women who carry guns[18]. Furthermore, misuse of firearms by the millions of American carry permit holders has proven to be virtually nil. It appears *hoplophobic*[20] journalists may be more susceptible to road rage fantasies than real gun owners are.

3. The "Guns are Dangerous to Their Owners" Lie

Professor Lott quotes surveys that indicate ninety-eight percent of the time people use guns defensively, they merely need to brandish them before a criminal to stop the inevitable attack. According to Lott, fifteen national polls, including those conducted by The Los Angeles Times and Gallup, record between 760,000 and 3.5 million defensive uses of guns per year. Florida State University Department of Criminology Professor Gary Kleck conducted a survey in 1993 which found 2.5 million crimes are thwarted each year by gun-owning Americans. His National Self-Defense Survey excluded cases where people picked up a gun to investigate

---

[18] As this article was being completed, the annual Puerto Rican Day Parade took place in New York City on June 11, 2000. Following the event more than 50 women filed complaints of sexual assault against some 60 men. Allegations that police stood idly by as the attacks took place rocked the media and led New York's then-Mayor Rudy Giuliani to proclaim that heads would roll. Imagine if just one of those women had been properly armed. Sixty drunken misogynists would have run like rabbits. Such an outrage is most unlikely to occur in the 31 of 50 states that enjoy "shall issue" concealed weapons permit laws.

[19] "I coined the term *hoplophobia*... in the sincere belief that we should recognize a very peculiar sociological attitude for what it is–a more or less hysterical neurosis rather than a legitimate political position. It follows convention in the use of Greek roots in describing specific mental afflictions. *Hoplon* is the Greek word for 'instrument; but refers synonymously to 'weapon' since the earliest and principal instruments were weapons. Phobos is Greek for 'terror' and medically denotes unreasoning panic rather than normal fear. Thus hoplophobia is a mental disturbance characterized by irrational aversion to weapons, as opposed to justified apprehension about those who may wield them:' (Quote from Cooper, Jeff. *To Ride, Shoot Straight, and Speak the Truth*. Wisdom Publishing, p. 16.)

suspicious noises and the like, and focused on actual confrontations between the intended victim and the offender.[20]

4. The "Success of the Brady Law" Lie

That the Clinton/Gore Administration boasted half a million people have been stopped by Brady Law background checks creates an interesting case of cognitive dissonance. Like those amazing body counts reported by the press during the Vietnam War, that if added together would have accounted for the population of India, there seems an inherent mathematical flaw. If half a million people committed the felony of illegally attempting to purchase a weapon when they were already legally banned from such actions by Federal law, why have there been merely a dozen arrests?[21]

5. The "Gun Show Loophole" Lie

The dreaded Gun Show loophole fretted over by the media and civilian disarmament proponents is a complete sham. If a person is engaged in gun dealing for profitable purposes, they need to have a Federal Firearms License to do so or they are committing a felony. If an FPL dealer sells a firearm at a gun show, the exact same laws apply as if they sold it out a store or home. In other words, identification provided by the buyer, Form 4473 filled out, a background check, and complete record keeping including make model and serial number of the weapon purchased.

---

[20] LaPierre, Wayne. *Guns, Crime and Freedom*. Regnery Publishing, 1994, p. 23.
[21] According to the statistics quoted by Wayne LaPierre in the April 2000 official NRA publication, *The American Rifleman*.

Question: What is the famous "Gun Show Loophole?"
Answer: Private sales that take place at Gun Shows.

In other words, as a gun owner I might want to trade up to a new rifle. Knowing a gun show was to be in town, I might put a little flag in the barrel of my old rifle with a "For Sale" written on it. I would have my gun checked by the police at the door, a trigger lock put on it, and hopefully find someone else looking for a bargain. After examining and recording each other's driver's licenses to verify it was an in-state sale and therefore not in violation of the 1968 Gun Control Act, and asking my buyer if he or she is a felon (and determining to the best of my ability that he is not), and therefore not subjecting myself to a ten-year prison sentence for selling to a felon, fugitive or drug user, we would conclude the transaction. Alternately, if I died and my wife wanted to raise some cash to bury my dead ass, she might take a couple of my guns to a gun show, rent a table, and try to sell them for a decent price. If she was earning a living from this, she would be a felon. However, if she was truly making private sales it would be legal in most states.

What the civilian disarmament lobby wants to do is make sure every gun is registered, and every transfer is recorded. That way, when they achieve the power to round up guns in private hands, they'll have everyone's address and know exactly what everyone owns. One of their key sophistries is that since cars are registered, why not register guns? However, unlike cars, boats or airplanes, the possession of firearms is specifically enumerated as a right of *the people*-a right protected from infringement by the same Government that registers cars.

6. The "Other Countries Have Better Gun Laws" Lie

To begin, I agree with Camille Paglia's sentiment, Neither do crime statistics from other countries carry much weight with me. Only the U.S. has a complex Bill of Rights with a First Amendment guaranteeing 'freedom of speech' and a Second Amendment guaranteeing 'the right of the people to keep and bear arms' which remain our protection against government tyranny. It's no coincidence that this most heavily armed nation in the world is also the most individualistic and entrepreneurial, with incandescent creativity in the high-tech field that has transformed the economy.

Other English-speaking countries have not improved their societies as much as the major news organizations would like us to believe. Dr. Miquel Faria Jr. informs us that the Australian crime rate is increasing exponentially following their infamous 1996 gun ban. In 1998, the first year after implementation of the ban, the Australian crime rate experienced a 44 percent increase in armed robberies, an 8.6 percent increase in aggravated assault, and a 3.2 percent increase in homicides. In the state of Victoria, there was a 300 percent increase in the number of homicides committed with a firearm. In South Australia, robberies increased by nearly 60 percent. In 1999, armed robberies in Australia were up 73 percent, unarmed robberies increased by 28 percent, kidnappings 38 percent, assaults by 17 percent, and manslaughter by 29 percent. During the previous 25 years before banning firearms, Australia enjoyed a steady decrease in the rate of both homicides with firearms and armed robbery.[22]

---

[22] Faria, Miquel Jr., M.D., Editor-in-Chief of *The Medical Sentinel*, the official publication of the Association of American Physicians and Surgeons. "Gun Control in Australia-Chaos Down Under'.' *The New American*, 22 May 2000.

England has not done much better. After Britain's even more stringent gun control laws were enacted in 1996, the 1998 armed crime rate grew 10 percent throughout 1997 despite a 19 percent decrease in the number of registered firearms. *The London Sunday Times* for January 16, 2000 estimated upward of three million illegal guns circulating in Britain. In some areas, the Times estimated as many of one-third of criminals from fifteen- to twenty-five-years-old owned or have access to firearms.[23] In Canada and Britain, almost half of all burglaries take place when the occupants are at home. In the better armed United States, only 13 percent of burglaries are perpetrated by those brave or foolish enough to take that risk[24].

GUNS AND RACE

America's first state and local gun laws were nearly all designed to keep guns out of the hands of slaves. These included laws passed prior to the American Revolution. After the Civil War, nearly every American gun law sought to keep guns out of the hands of freed former slaves. Thus gun control has always had a particularly odious racial cast. However this is also true to an alarming degree of crime.

The Welfare State has failed miserably. In four decades, it has created a permanent crime-ridden under class whose family structure has been destroyed by regulations that encourage out-of-wedlock births and social and political policies that 1) pay people not to work, and 2) export unskilled labor manufacturing jobs overseas. Thus America has created an alternate inner city sub-culture that serves as both a permanent threat to social well-being, and an object lesson in collectivism. Yet it also serves to provide statistics for the civilian disarmament movement. The horrific crime rate among inner city poor allows for the assertion that guns kill

---
[23] Lee, Robert W. "English Crime Rate" *The New American,* 24 April 2000.
[24] Lott, John Jr. *More Guns, Less Crime.* University of Chicago Press, 1998, p. 5.

people who simply cannot be trusted to own a twenty-ounce mechanical device; that somehow, these objects seem to exert a mysterious force–especially on the psyche of America's racial minorities. This is the justification behind the crippling spate of lawsuits filed against the gun industry by big city mayors and the Department of Housing and Urban Development. Rather than leading a chorus of outrage against this insidious racial insult, the left-wing National Association for the Advancement of Colored People (NAACP) has threatened its own lawsuit against the gun industry because of the "disproportionate" effect of gun violence in the black community.

On the other hand, there is an appalling amount of black crime. According to Department of Justice figures compiled for 1997, the incidence of black crime is proportionately far greater than white. A reasonable similarity appears to exist between crime figures and arrest figures. For example, according to the Department of Justice survey for 1997, 60 percent of robberies were reported to have been committed by blacks, while 57 percent of those arrested for robberies were black.[25] The FBI Uniform Crime Report for 1992 found 55 percent of those arrested for murder were black, while 43.4 percent of murder victims were also black. The FBI found that in 1992, 94 percent of black victims were slain by black assailants[26]. Thus, when gun control advocates talk of banning "cheap handguns;' the result of their efforts, if successful, will be to leave poor people in high crime areas defenseless. Ironically, it seems modern efforts at gun control are as unconscionably racist as earlier gun control policies.[27]

---

[25] Taylor, Jared. "What Color is Crime?" *The Resister*,Vol. 5, No. 3, Summer/Autumn 1999.
[26] Bolton, John. "Counter-Propaganda 101:' *The Resister*, Vol. 4, No. 2, Winter 1998.
[27] Conversely, the Department of Justice figures for interracial crime in 1994 report that 89 percent of single offender crimes and 94 percent of multiple offender crimes were committed by blacks against whites. If these figures are rendered as violent crime per 100,000, 3,494 blacks out of 100,000 committed a violent crime against a white person in 1994, while 64 whites out of a 100,000 committed a violent crime against a black person. (Statistics from Taylor, Jared. "What Color is Crime?" *The Resister*, Vol. 5, No. 3, Summer/Autumn 1999.)

As a law-abiding American citizen who lives in a normal environment, I refuse to be treated like some seventeen-year-old, out of control, inner city gang banger, hopped up on crack, and suffering from a dearth of moral values. My children and I were raised to exhibit both the respect for life and personal self-control required to enjoy the freedom to keep and bear arms.

ALARMING PRECEDENTS FOR NATIONAL GUN REGISTRATION

From 1789 to 1934 there was not one federal gun law-with the exception of the Second Amendment. The first unconstitutional gun law was passed as the 1934 National Firearms Act which sought to ban automatic weapons by burdening them with heavy taxes and unprecedented registration requirements. The next one was the 1968 Gun Control Act, modeled nearly word for word after gun laws enacted by the Nazi regime.

The Nazis inherited the German 1928 Law on Firearms and Ammunition which required registration and renewable permits for firearm owners and their firearms, mandated permits for the acquisitions of ammunition, and the issuance of hunting permits. All firearms had to be stamped with serial numbers and the names of their manufacturers. When the Nazis came to power in 1933, they thus had access to the name and home address of every legal gun owner in Germany, along with a description of their weapons.

The Nazi Weapons Law of 1938 guaranteed only friends of the Nazi Party could own and carry firearms. Jews of course were forbidden to own guns or to participate in any business dealing in weapons. Carry permits were required in order to bear arms and were only issued to "persons of undoubted reliability, and only if a demonstration of need is set forth.

In *Gun Control: Gateway to Tyranny*, Jay Simpkin and Aaron Zelman lay out the 1938 Nazi Weapons Law with a paragraph by paragraph comparison to the U.S. Gun Control Act of 1968.[29] Anyone interested in seeking the basis for U.S. gun control legislation is recommended to make this fearless comparison. The authors also present documentary evidence that Senator Thomas Dodd (D-CT), one of the authors of the 1968 law, had several months earlier submitted official requests to the Library of Congress for an English translation of the 1938 Nazi Weapons Law.

GUN CONTROL DOES WORK TO ACCOMPLISH THE WRONG RESULTS

Gun Control is a successful mechanism for the establishment of tyranny. Between 75 and 86 million Americans own between 200 million and 240 million guns[30]. Who is going to check that each one of these guns is properly registered by each of these gun owners? Who is going to come into your house to insure a gun lock is installed on your weapon? Do you want your neighbor encouraged to inspect your home to determine how you store your gun before allowing their children to play with yours? Should your kids be programmed to report your guns to the D.A.R.E officer in their schools? Given the nature of people, if all guns mysteriously disappeared into thin air, would the rates of murder, assault and suicide really decline?

---

[29] Simpkin, Jay and Zelma, Aaron, both of Jews For the Preservation of Firearm Ownership. "Gun Control: Gateway to Tyranny;' 1993.
[30] Lott, John Jr. *More Guns, Less Crime*. University of Chicago Press, 1998.

Pop Quiz: Was the War on Drugs more effective in: a) limiting the manufacture, availability, and use of drugs, or b) filling our nations prisons while extending the powers of the Police State?

My advice to any reader who still values his or her freedom, and continues to assert the sacred right of self-preservation, is to make the effort to familiarize yourself with guns. Take the time and training required to learn to use a gun well. Once you are comfortable enough to make a choice, buy a good one and practice with it. Join the NRA immediately and contribute regularly. Speak to your friends, family and neighbors.

Make phone calls and send letters to politicians. Remind them you intend to hold their feet to the fire of the Constitution. No matter how many people tell you otherwise, the Constitution is still the law of the land. Consider the next time you hear some media sycophant drooling about the "international community" that our freedoms are unique to America. Each one of us had better be an active advocate of Liberty-otherwise, Liberty will vanish.

William S. Burroughs describes the title of his novel *Naked Lunch* as "a frozen moment when everyone sees what is on the end of every fork." I therefore make the following recommendation to anyone who plans to vote for any politician who endorses gun control. First, burn a copy of the Bill of Rights. Then pull the lever to cast your vote. That way, at least you can say you had the courage to acknowledge the future you were creating.

JANUARY 13, 2011:

Just as this book was going to press, a mass shooting occurred in Tucson, Arizona in which a Democrat House member was severely wounded, and a Republican judge and young girl killed along with several others. A mad man was responsible and a photo of him basking in his media notoriety was soon broadcast worldwide. Even faster than the release of the photo, however-within just two hours of the shooting-a Nobel prize-winning moron from *The New York Times* blamed talk radio and the Tea Party.

Later that day, a half-witted Arizona county sheriff attempted to cover his tracks by blaming those who rejected Obama's takeover of healthcare. We then learned the murderer had made at least five death threats investigated and ignored by the sheriff's department. Statistics of the sheriff's poor crime fighting record emerged. Because law enforcement had not properly referred the perpetrator to mental health authorities, the killer was able to pass an FBI background check and purchase his weapon.

The shooting was referred to as a "tragedy." It was not a tragedy. It was an outrage, a crime, an obscenity. The tragedy was that left wing media outlets and corrupt politicians were trying to get away with blaming adult political discourse for the behavior of a lunatic. Before the blood was dry, Democrat Carolyn McCarthy was introducing anti-gun legislation so the rest of us could be as defenseless as her husband-killed on the Long Island Railroad by a black racist in 1993—or the unarmed Virginia Tech students in 2007. So tedious. Yet, we go forth on.

OSHO Bhagwan Shree Rajneesh
Enlightened Master, Teacher and One of the
Greatest Religious Leaders of All Time

REBELLION IS THE BIGGEST "YES" YET

OSHO (Bhagwan Shree Rajneesh)

Author of the New Falcon Publication title:
Rebellion, Revolution & Religiousness

Beloved Master. All the historical rebellions have a huge "no" at their source. Your rebellion of the soul is centered in the mystery of "Yes." *Will you please speak to us on the alchemy of "Yes"?*

There are a few very fundamental things to be understood.

First, there has never been a rebellion in the past, only revolutions. And the distinction between a revolution and a rebellion is so vast that unless you understand the difference you will not be able to figure the way out of the puzzle of your question. Once you understand the difference...

Revolution is a crowd, a mob phenomenon. Revolution is a struggle for power: one class of people who are in power are thrown out by the other class of people who have been oppressed, exploited to such a point that now even death does not matter. They don't have anything. Revolution is a struggle between the haves and have-nots.

I am reminded of the last statement in the Communist Manifesto by Karl Marx. It is tremendously beautiful, and with a little change I can use it for my own purposes.

First its exact statement: he says, "Proletariate"–his word for the have-nots–Proletariat of the world unite, and don't be afraid because you have nothing to lose except your chains."

Moments come in history when a small group of people–cunning, clever–start exploiting the whole society. All the money goes on gathering on one side and all the poverty and starvation on the other. Naturally this state cannot be continued forever. Sooner or later those who have nothing are going to overthrow those who have all.

Revolution is a class action, it is a class struggle. It is basically political; it has nothing to do with religion, nothing to do with spirituality. And it is also violent, because those who have power are not going to lose their vested interest easily; it is going to be a bloody, violent struggle in which thousands, sometimes millions of people will die.

Just in the Russian Revolution thirty million people were killed. The czar's whole family–he was the king of Russia before the revolution–was killed by the revolutionaries so brutally that it is inconceivable. Even a six-month-old girl was also killed. Now, she was absolutely innocent, she had done no harm to anybody; but just because she belonged to the royal family... The whole royal family had to be destroyed completely. Seventeen people were killed, and not just killed but cut into pieces.

It is bound to happen in a revolution. Centuries of anger ultimately turn into blind violence.

And the last thing to remember: revolution changes nothing. It is a wheel: one class comes into power, others become powerless. But sooner or later the powerless are going to become the majority, because the powerful don't want to share their power, they want to have it in as few hands as possible.

Now, you cannot conceive in this country... There are nine hundred million people, but half the capital of the country is just in Bombay. Nine hundred million people in the whole country, and half the capital of the whole country is just in a small city. How long can it be tolerated? Revolution comes naturally, automatically–it is sometimes blind and mechanical, part of evolution. And when the powerful become the smaller group, the majority throws them away and another power group starts doing the same.

That's why I say revolution has never changed anything, or in other words, all the revolutions of history have failed. They promised much, but nothing came out of it. Even after seventy years, in the Soviet Union people are still not getting enough nourishment. Yes, there are no more the old czars and counts and countesses and princesses and princes–but in a vast ocean of poverty, even if you remove those who have power and riches it is not going to make the society rich; it is just like trying to make the ocean sweet by dropping teaspoonfuls of sugar in it.

All that has happened is a very strange phenomenon that nobody takes notice of. Only, poverty has been distributed equally: now in the Soviet Union everybody is equally poor. But what kind of revolution is this? The hope was that everybody would be equally rich.

But just by hoping you cannot become rich. Richness needs a totally different ideology of which mankind is absolutely unaware. For centuries it has praised poverty and condemned richness, comfort, luxury. Even it the poor revolt and come into power, they don't have any idea what to do with this power, how to generate energy to create more richness, comfort and luxury for the people. Because deep down in their minds there is a guilty feeling about richness, about luxury, about comfort.

So they are in a tremendous anguish, although they have come to power. This is the moment they could change the whole structure of the society, its whole productive idea.

They could bring more technology; they could drop stupid kinds of wastage.

Every country is wasting almost ten percent of its income on the army. Even the poorest country, even this country is doing the same idiotic thing. Fifty percent of the people in this country are on the verge of any day becoming an Ethiopia, a bigger Ethiopia. In Ethiopia one thousand people were dying per day. The day India starts becoming another Ethiopia–and it is not far away–then one thousand will not do; it will be many thousands of people dying every day.

By the end of this century the population of India will be the biggest in the whole world. So far it has never been; it has always been China that was ahead. By the end of the century–and there are not many years left, just within twelve years we will be reaching the end–India will have one billion people. Five hundred million people are bound to die, because there is no food for so many people.

But still the politicians, those who are in power, are not concerned at all what happens to humanity. Their concern is whether power remains in their hands or not. The can sacrifice half of the country, but they will go on making efforts to have atomic weapons, nuclear missiles.

It is a very insane kind of society that we have created in thousands of years. Its insanity has come now to a high peak. There is no going back. It seems we are all sitting on a volcano which can explode any moment.

Revolutions in the past have happened all around the world, but no revolution has succeeded in doing what it promised. It promised equality, without understanding the psychology of human individuality. Each human individual is so unique that to force them to equality is not going to make people happy, but utterly miserable.

OSHO Bhagwan Shree, known as one of the most famous, and to some, infamous, religious leaders of modern times.

I also love the idea of equality, but in a totally different way. My idea of equality is equal opportunity for all to be unique and themselves. Certainly they will be different from each other, and a society which does not have variety and differences is a very poor society. Variety brings beauty, richness, color.

But it has not yet dawned on the millions around the world that revolution has not helped, and they still go on thinking in terms of revolution. The have not understood anything from the history of man.

It is said that history repeats itself. I say it is not history that repeats itself; it only seems to repeat itself because man is absolutely unconscious and he goes on doing the same thing again and again without learning anything, without becoming mature, alert and aware.

When all the revolutions have failed some new door should be opened. There is no point in again and again changing the powerful into the powerless and the powerless into the powerful; this is a circle that goes on moving.

I don't preach revolution.

I am utterly against revolution.

I say unto you that my word for the future, and for those who are intelligent enough in the present, is *rebellion*.

What is the difference?

Rebellion is individual action; it has nothing to do with the crowd. Rebellion has nothing to do with politics, power, violence. Rebellion has something to do with changing your consciousness, your silence, your being. It is a spiritual metamorphosis.

And each individual passing through a rebellion is not fighting with anybody else, but is fighting only with his own darkness. Swords are not needed, bombs are not needed; what is needed is more alertness, more meditativeness, more love, more prayerfulness, more gratitude. Surrounded by all these qualities you are born anew.

I teach this new man, and this rebellion can become the womb for the new man I teach. We have tried collective efforts and they have failed. Now let us try individual efforts. And if one man becomes aflame with consciousness, joy and blissfulness, he will become contagious to many more.

Rebellion is a very silent phenomenon that will go on spreading without making any noise and without even leaving any footprints behind. It will move from heart to heart in deep silences, and the day it has reached to millions of people without any bloodshed, just the understanding of those millions of people will change our old primitive animalistic ways.

It will change our greed, and the day greed is gone there is no question of accumulating money. No revolution has been able to destroy greed; those who come into power become greedy.

We have passed through a revolution just now in this

country, and it is a very significant example to understand. The people who were leading the revolution in this country against the British rule were followers of Mahatma Gandhi, who preached poverty, who preached non-possessiveness. The moment they came into power all his disciples started living in palaces which were made for viceroys. All his disciples who had been thinking their whole lives that they are servants of the people became masters of the people.

There is more corruption in this country than anywhere else. This is very strange–this is Gandhian corruption, very religious, very pious, and the people who are doing it were trained, disciplined to be servants of the people. But power has a tremendous capacity to change people; the moment you have power you are immediately a different person. You start behaving exactly like any other powerful person who have gone before.

Nothing has changed. Only the British are gone, and in their place a single party has been ruling for forty years. Now it is not just a single party, but a single family; it has become a dynasty. And the exploitation continues and the poverty continues–it has grown at least a hundred times more since the British Empire has been gone.

Everything has deteriorated–the morality, the character, the integrity, everything has become a commodity. You can purchase anybody; all you need is money. There is not a single individual in the whole country who is not a commodity in the marketplace; all you need is money. Everybody is purchasable–judges are purchasable, police commissioners are purchasable, politicians are purchasable. Even under the British rule this country has never known such corruption.

What has the country gained? The rulers have changed, but what does this signify? Unless there is a rebelliousness spreading from individual to individual, unless we can create an atmosphere of enlightenment around the world where greed will fall down on its own accord, where anger will not be possible, where violence will become impossible, where love will be just the way you live...where life should be respected, where the boy should be loved, appreciated, where comfort should not be condemned. It is natural to ask for comfort.

Even the trees... In Africa, trees grow very high; the same trees in India don't grow that high. I was puzzled, what happens? I was trying to find out why they should grow to the same height but they don't, and the reason I found was that unless there is a density of trees, trees won't grow high. Even at a lesser height the sun is available, and that is their comfort, that is their life, that is their joy. In Africa the jungles are so thick that every tree tries in every way to grow as high as possible, because only then can it have the joy of the sun, the joy of the rain, the joy of the wind. Only then can it dance; otherwise the is nothing but death.

The whole of nature wants comfort, the whole of nature wants all the luxury that is possible. But our religions have been teaching us against luxury, against comfort, against riches.

A man of enlightenment sees with clarity that is it unnatural to demand from people, "You should be content with your poverty, you should be content with your sicknesses, you should be content with all kinds of exploitation, you should be content and you should not try to rise higher, to reach to the sun and the rain and the wind." This is absolutely unnatural conditioning that we are all carrying. Only a rebellion in your being can bring you to this clarity.

You say that in history all the rebellions were based on "no." Those were not rebellions; change the word. All the revolutions were based on "no." They were negative, they were against something, they were destructive, they were revengeful and violent.

Certainly, my rebellion is based on "yes"–yes to existence, yes to nature, yes to yourself. Whatever the religions may be saying and whatever the ancient traditions may be saying, they are all saying no to yourself, no to nature, no to existence; they are all life-negative.

My rebellion is life-affirmative. I want you to dance and sing and love and live as intensely as possible and as totally as possible. In this total affirmation of life, in this absolute "yes" to nature we can bring a totally new earth and a totally new humanity into being.

The past was "no."

The future has to be "yes."

We have lived enough with the "no," we have suffered enough and there has been nothing but misery. I want people to be as joyful as birds singing in the morning, as colorful as flowers, as free as the bird on the wing with no bondages, with no conditioning, with no past–just an open future, an open sky and you can fly to the stars.

Because I am saying yes to life, all the no-sayers are against me, all over the world. My yes-saying goes against all the religions and against all the ideologies that have been forced upon man. My "yes" is my rebellion. The day you will also be able to say "yes" it will be your rebellion.

We can have rebellious people functioning together, but each will be an independent individual, not belonging to a political party or to a religious organization. Just out of freedom and out of love and out of the same beautiful "yes" we will meet. Our meeting will not be a contract, our meeting will not be in any way a surrender; our meeting will make every individual more individual. Supported by everybody else, our meeting will not take away freedom, will not enslave you; our meeting will give you more freedom, more support so that you can be stronger in your freedom. Long has been the slavery, and long has been our burden. We have become weak because of the thousands of years of darkness that have been poured on us.

The people who love to say "yes" who understand the meaning of rebellion, will not be alone; they will be individuals. But the people who are on the same path, fellow-travelers, friends, will be supporting each other in their meditativeness, in their joy, in their dance, in their music. They will become a spiritual orchestra, where so many people are playing instruments but creating one music. So many people can be together and yet they may be creating the same consciousness, the same light, the same joy, the same fragrance.

It is a long way– "no" seems to be a shortcut–that's why it has not been tried up to now. Whenever I have discussed it with people, they said, "Perhaps you are right, but when will it be possible that the whole earth will say 'yes'?"

I said, "Anyway we have been on this earth for millions of years and you have been saying 'no'–and what is your achievement? It is time. Give a chance to 'yes' too."

My feeling is that "no" is a quality of death; "yes" is the very center of life. "No" had to fail because death cannot succeed, cannot be victorious over life. If we give a chance to "yes" based in rebelliousness it is bound to become a wildfire, because everybody deep down wants it to happen. I have not found a single person in my life who does not want to live a natural, relaxed peaceful, silent life.

But that life is possible only if everybody else is also living the same kind of life.

I can understand the fear of people that individual rebellion may take a long time, but there is no problem in it.

In fact each individual who passes through this rebellious fire becomes at least for himself a bliss and an ecstasy, and there is every possibility that he will sow the seeds around him. But he has not failed; he has conquered, he has reached to the very peak of his potential. He has blossomed. There is nothing more that he can think of; the whole existence is his.

So as far as that individual is concerned the rebellion is complete. He will be able to sow seeds all around. And there is no hurry; eternity is available. Slowly, slowly more and more people will become more and more conscious, more alert. Enlightenment will become a common phenomenon.

It should not be that only in a while there is a Gautam Buddha, once in a while there is a Jesus, once in a while there is a Socrates–the names can be counted on only ten fingers. This is simply unbelievable. It is as if our garden is full of rosebushes, thousands of rosebushes, and once in a while one rosebush blossoms and gives you roses. And the remaining thousands remain without flowers?

Unless a rosebush comes to blossom it cannot dance– for what? It cannot share; it has nothing to share. It remains poor, empty, meaningless. Whether it lived or not makes no difference.

The only difference is that when it blossoms and offers its songs and its flowers and its fragrance to existence and to anybody who is willing to receive, the rosebush is fulfilled. Its life has not been just a meaningless drag; it has become a beautiful dance full of songs, a deep fulfillment that goes to the very roots.

I am not worried about time. If the concept is understood, time is available; enough time is available.

In the East we have a beautiful proverb: The man who loses the path in the morning, if he returns home by evening he should not be called lost. What does it matter? In the morning he went astray–just little adventures here and there–and by the evening he is back home. A few people may have come a little earlier; he has come a little late, but he is not necessarily poorer than those who have come earlier. It may be just vice versa: he may be more experienced because he has gone wandering so far astray. And then coming back again, falling and getting up–he is not necessarily a loser.

So time is not at all a consideration to me.

My rebellion is absolutely individual and it will spread from individual to individual. Sometime this whole planet is bound to become enlightened. Idiots may try to wait and see what happens to others, but they also finally have to join the caravan.

The very idea of enlightenment is so new, although it is not something that has not been known before. There have been enlightened people, but they never brought enlightenment as a rebellion. That is what is new about it. They became enlightened, they became contented, they became fulfilled, and a great fallacy happened and I have to point it out. Although I feel not to show any mistakes of the enlightened ones–I feel sad about it–but my responsibility is not for the dead. My responsibility is for those who are alive and for those who will be coming.

So I have to make it clear. Gautam Buddha, Mahavira, Adinatha, Lao Tzu, Kabir, all those people who became enlightened attained to tremendous beauty, to great joy, to utter ecstasy–to what I have been calling *satyam, shivam, sundram*, the truth, the godliness of the truth and the beauty of that godliness.

But because they had become enlightened they started teaching people to be contented: "Remain peaceful, remain silent." This is the fallacy. They attained contentment after a long search. It was a conclusion, not a beginning; it was the very end product of their enlightenment, but they started telling people that you can be contented right now: "Be fulfilled, be silent."

That's how they became anti-rebellious, without perhaps knowing that if a poor man remains contented with his poverty it is dangerous; if a slave remains contented with his slavery, it is dangerous.

So all the enlightened people of the past attained to great heights, about which there is no doubt. But there is a fallacy that they all perpetuated without exception. The fallacy is that they began telling people to start with that which comes in the end. The flower comes only in the end; one has to start with the roots, with the seed. And if you tell people to start with the roses, then the only way is to purchase roses of plastic. The only way to be contented without meditation is to be a hypocrite, because deep down you are angry, deep down you are furious, deep down you want to freak out, and on the surface you are showing immense peace. This peace has been like a cancer to humanity.

You can see it happening in this country more clearly than anywhere else, because this country was fortunate, blessed by more enlightened people than any other country– but unfortunately, because so many enlightened people committed the same fallacy, this country remained for twenty centuries continuously a slave.

"Hallelujah! Came the response from the back.

The vicar managed to get to the end of the sermon, but at the end went up to the American and said, "Excuse me, I'm afraid in this country we like to keep a bit of decorum. We try to keep a stiff upper lip. It is the queen's own country, this is a place of God, and I frankly found your behavior rather disconcerting."

"Hey, man, I'm sorry, you are right on. I just loved the quaint way you gave us all that great shit about Moses and the Ten Commandments and I thought I would throw a few thousand greenbacks in your direction for this great thing going on here."

"Cool, man!" said the preacher.

It does not take much to find out what is deep inside. All decorum, all culture is so superficial; it will be a tremendous joy to see people in their authenticity, in their reality, without any decorum, without any make-up, just as they are. The world will be tremendously benefited if all this falseness disappears.

The alchemy of "yes" and the rebellion based on "yes" are capable of destroying all that is false, and discovering all that is real and has been covered for centuries, layer upon layer by every generation, so much that even you yourself have forgotten who you are.

If suddenly somebody wakes you up in the middle of the night and asks you, "Who are you?" you will take a little time to remember who you used to be the night before when you went to bed.

It happened that George Bernard Shaw was going to deliver a lecture some distance away from London. On the way in the train came the ticket-checker. George Bernard Shaw looked in every pocket, opened all his suitcases, but the ticket was not there. Finally, he was perspiring and the ticket-checker said, "Don't be worried, I know who you are; the whole country knows, the whole world knows. The ticket must be somewhere, you don't be worried. And even if its lost, I am here to help you get out of the station, wherever you want to get out."

George Bernard Shaw said, "Shut up! I am already in confusion and you are making me more confused. I am trying to remember where I am going! That ticket was the only thing…I am not searching for the ticket for you, idiot; I don't care about you, you can get lost. Bring me my ticket!"

The man said, "But how can I find your ticket?"

George Bernard Shaw said, "Then what am I supposed to do? Where should I get down? Because unless I know the name of the station…"

It is almost the same situation with everybody. You don't know who you are; your name is just a label that has been put upon you, it is not your being. Where are you going?– you don't have any ticket to show you where you are going to get down, and you are just hoping that somebody may push you somewhere, or maybe somewhere the terminus comes and the train stops and it does not go anywhere else… Just hoping.

But why are you traveling in the first place? In fact, for all those fundamental questions you have only one answer: I don't know. In this state of unawareness your revolutions cannot succeed. In this state of unawareness, your desire for freedom is just a dream. You cannot understand what freedom is. For whom are you asking freedom?

My idea of a rebellion based on "yes' means a rebellion based on meditation, for the first time in the history of man. And because each individual has to work upon himself, there is no question of any fight, there is no question of any organization, there is no question of any conspiracy, there is no question of planting bombs and hijacking airplanes.

I am not interested in hijacking airplanes, neither am I interested in destroying any governments. But it will be the final result of my individual rebellion based on meditation: government will disappear. They have to disappear; they have been nothing by a nuisance on the earth. Nations have to disappear. There is no need of any nations; the whole earth belongs to the whole of humanity. There is no need of any passports, there is no need of any visas.

This earth is ours, and what kind of freedom is there if we cannot even move? Everywhere there are barriers, every nation is a big imprisonment. Just because you cannot see the boundaries you think you are free. Just try to pass through the boundary and immediately you will be faced with a loaded gun: "Go back inside the prison. You belong in prison. You cannot enter into another prison without permission." These are your nations!

Certainly, a rebellion of my vision will take away all this garbage of nations, and discrimination between white and black, and give the whole of humanity a natural, relaxed, comfortable life. This is possible, because science has given us everything that we need, even if the population of the earth is three times more than it is today.

Just a little intelligence is needed–which will be released by meditation–and we can have a beautiful earth with beautiful people, and a multidimensional freedom which is not just a word in the dead constitution books but a living reality.

One thing finally to be remembered: the days of revolution are past. We have tried them many times, and every time the same story is repeated. Enough. Now something new is urgently needed. And except for the idea that I am giving you of a rebellion, individual and based on meditativeness, there is no other alternative proposed anywhere in the world.

And I am not a philosopher; I am absolutely pragmatic and practical. I am not only talking about meditative rebellion, I am preparing people for it. Whether you know it or not doesn't matter. Whoever comes close to me is going to become a rebellious individual, and wherever he will go he will spread this contagious health. It will make people aware of their dignity, it will make people aware of their potentiality. It will make people alert to what they can become, what they are, and why they are stuck.

My sannyasins' function is not to be missionaries, but to be so loving, compassionate, such fragrant individuals... It is not a question of converting people from one ideology to another ideology. It is a far deeper transformation–from the whole past to a totally new and unknown future. It is the greatest adventure that one can think of.

Satyam-Shivam-Sundram, Session 26, Nov. 19, 1987

Timothy Leary, Ph.D.
World famous Psychologist, Writer and Philosopher

The authors divide the stages of human history into: tribal, feudal, industrial, and cybernetic. The arrival of the latter stage is heralded in the authors' book *Cybernetic Societies*.

TWENTY-TWO ALTERNATIVES TO INVOLUNTARY DEATH

Timothy Leary, Ph.D. & Eric Gullichsen

Author of the New Falcon Publication title:
What Does WoMan Want?
The Intelligence Agents
The Game of Life
Info-Psychology
Neuropolitique

"Death is the ultimate negative patient health outcome."
–William L. Roper, Director, Health Care Financing Administration (HCFA), which administers Medicare

Most human beings face death with an "attitude" of helplessness, either resigned or fearful. Neither of these submissive, often uninformed, "angles of approach" to the most crucial event of one's life can be ennobling.

Today, there are many practical options available for dealing with dying process. Passivity, failure to learn about them, might be the ultimate irretrievable blunder. Pascal's famous no-lose wager about the existence of God translates into modern life as a no-risk gamble on the prowess of technology.

For millennia the fear of death has depreciated individual confidence and increased dependence on authority.

True, the loyal member of a familial or racial gene-pool can take pride in the successes and survival tenacity of their kinship. But for the individual, the traditional prospects are less than exalted. Let's be laser-honest here. How can you be proud of your past achievements, walk tall in the present or zap enthusiastically into the future if, awaiting you implacably around some future corner, is Old Mr. D., The Grim Reaper?

What a PR job the Word Makers did to build this Death Concept into a Prime-Time Horror Show! The grave. Mortification. Extinction. Breakdown. Catastrophe. Doom. Finish. Fatality. Malignancy. Necrology. Obituary. The end.

Note the calculated negativity. To die is to croak, to give up the ghost, to bite the dust, to kick the bucket, to perish. To become inanimate, lifeless, defunct, extinct, moribund, cadaverous, necrotic. A corpse, a stiff, a cadaver, a relic, food for worms, a *corpus delicti*, a carcass. What a miserable ending to the game of life!

Fear Of Death Was An Evolutionary Necessity In The Past

In the past, the reflexive genetic duty of TOP MANAGEMENT (those in social control of the various gene-pools) has been to make humans feel weak, helpless, and dependent in the face of death. The good of the race or nation was ensured at the cost of the sacrifice of the individual.

Obedience and submission was rewarded on a time-payment plan. For his/her devotion the individual was promised immortality in the post-mortem hive-center variously known as "heaven," "paradise," or the "Kingdom of the Lord." In order to maintain the attitude of dedication, the gene-pool managers had to control the "dying reflexes," orchestrate the trigger-stimuli that activate the "death circuits" of the brain. This was accomplished through rituals that imprint dependence and docility when the "dying alarm bells" go off in the brain.

Perhaps we can better understand this imprinting mechanism by considering another set of "rituals," those by which human hives manage the conception-reproduction reflexes. A discussion of these is less likely to alarm you. And the mechanisms of control imposed by the operation of social machinery are similar in the two cases. We invite you to "step outside the system" for a moment, to vividly see what is ordinarily invisible because it is so entrenched in our expectation.

At adolescence each kinship group provides rituals, taboos, ethical prescriptions to guide the all-important sperm-egg situation.

Management by the individual of the horny DNA machinery is always a threat to hive inbreeding. Dress, grooming, dating, courtship, contraception, and abortion patterns are fanatically conventionalized in tribal and feudal societies. Personal innovation is sternly condemned and ostracized. Industrial democracies vary in the sexual freedom allowed individuals. But in totalitarian states, China and Iran for example, rigid prudish morality controls the mating reflexes and governs boy-girl relations. Under the Chinese dictator Mao, "romance" was forbidden because it weakened dedication to the state, i.e., the local gene-pool. If teenagers pilot and select their own mating, then they will be more likely to fertilize outside the hive, more likely to insist on directing their own lives, and, worst of all, less likely to rear their offspring with blind gene-pool loyalty.

Even more rigid social-imprinting rituals guard the "dying reflexes." Hive control of "death" responses is taken for granted in all pre-cybernetic societies.

In the past this conservative degradation of individuality was an evolutionary virtue.

During epochs of species stability, when the tribal, feudal and industrial technologies were being mastered and fine-tuned, wisdom was centered in the gene-pool stored in the collective linguistic-consciousness, the racial data-base of the hive.

Since individual life was short, brutish, aimless, what a singular learned was nearly irrelevant. The world was changing so slowly that knowledge could only be embodied in the species. Lacking the technologies for the personal mastery of transmission and storage of information, the individual was simply too slow, too small, to matter. Loyalty to the racial collective was the virtue. Creativity, Premature Individuation, was anti-evolutionary. A weirdo, mutant distraction. Only Village Idiots would try to commit independent, unauthorized thought.

In the feudal and industrial eras, Management used the fear of death to motivate and control individuals. Today, politicians use the death-dealing military and the police and capital punishment to protect the social order. Organized religion maintains its power and wealth by orchestrating and exaggerating the fear of death.

Among the many things that the Pope, the Ayatollah, and Fundamentalist Protestants agree on: confident understanding and self-directed mastery of the dying process is the last thing to be allowed to the individual. The very notion of *Cybernetic Post-Biological Intelligence* or consumer immortality-options is taboo, sinful. For formerly valid reasons of gene-pool protection.

Religions have cleverly monopolized the rituals of dying to increase control over the superstitious. Throughout history the priests and mullahs have swarmed around the expiring human like black vultures. Death belonging to them.

As we grow in the 20th century we are systematically programmed about How to Die. Hospitals are staffed with priests/ministers/rabbis ready to perform the "last rites."

Every army unit has its Catholic Chaplin to administer the Sacrament of Extreme Unction (what a phrase, really!) to the expiring solider. The Ayatollah, Chief Mullah of the Islamic Death Cult, sends his teenage soldiers into the Iraq mine fields with dog-tags guaranteeing immediate transfer to the Allah's Destination Resort. Koranic Heaven. A terrible auto crash? Call the medics! Call the priest! Call the Reverend!

In the Industrial Society, everything becomes part of Big Business. Dying involves Blue Cross, Medicare, Health Care Delivery Systems, the Health Care Financing Administration (HCFA), terminal patient wards. Undertakers. Cemeteries. The funeral rituals.

The monopolies of religion and the assembly lines of Top Management process dying and the dead even more efficiently than the living.

We recall that knowledge and selective choice about such gene-pool issues as conception, test-tube fertilization, pregnancy, abortion is dangerous enough to the church-fathers.

But suicide, right-to-die concepts, euthanasia, life extension, out-of-body-experiences, occult experimentation, astral-travel scenarios, death/rebirth reports, extraterrestrial speculation, cryogenics, sperm-banks, egg-banks, DNA banks, personally-empowering Artificial Intelligence Technology–anything that encourages the individual to engage in personal speculation and experimentation with immortality– is anathema to the orthodox Seed-Shepherds of the feudal and industrial ages.

Why? Because if the flock doesn't fear death, then the grip of Religious and Political Management is broken. The power of the gene-pool is threatened. And when control looses in the gene-pool, dangerous genetic innovations and mutational visions tend to emerge.

Some believe that the Cybernetic Age we are entering could mark the beginning of a period of enlightened and intelligent individualism, a time unique in history when technology is available to individuals to support a huge diversity of personalized lifestyles and cultures, a world of diverse, interacting social groups whose initial-founding membership number is one.

The exploding technology of computation and communication lays a delicious feast of knowledge and personal choice within our easy grasp. Under such conditions, the operating wisdom and control naturally passes from aeons-old power of gene pools, and locates in the rapidly self-modifying brains of individuals capable of dealing with an ever-accelerating rate of change.

Aided by customized, personally-programmed quantum-linguistic appliances, the individual can choose his/her own social genetic future. And perhaps choose not to "die."

The Wave Theory Of Evolution

Current theories of genetics suggest that evolution, like everything else in the universe, comes in waves.

So, at times of Punctuated Evolution, collective metamorphosis, when many things are mutating at the same time, then the ten commandments of the "old ones" become ten more suggestions...

At such times of rapid innovation and collective mutation, conservative hive dogma can be dangerous, suicidal. Individual experimentation and exploration, the thoughtful methodical scientific challenging of taboos, becomes the key to the survival of the gene-school.

Now, as we enter the Cybernetic Age, we arrive at a new wisdom which broadens our definition of personal immortality and gene-pool survival: *The Post-Biological Options Of The Information Species*. A fascinating set of gourmet-consumer choices suddenly appear on the pop-up menu of The Evolutionary Café.

It is beginning to look as though in the Information Society, the individual human being can script, produce, direct his/her own immortality.

Here we face Mutation Shock in its most panicky form. And, as we have done in understanding earlier mutations, the first step is to develop a new language. We should not impose our values or vocabulary of the past species upon the new Cybernetic Culture.

Would you let the buzz-words of a preliterate Paleolithic cult control your life? Will you let the superstitions of a tribal-village culture (now represented by the Pope and the Ayatollah) shuffle you off the scene? Will you let the mechanical planned obsolescence tactics of the Factory Culture manage your existence?

So let us have no more pious wimp-sheep talk about death. The time has come to talk cheerfully and joke sassily about personal responsibility for managing the dying process. For starters let's de-mystify death and develop alternative metaphors for consciousness leaving the body. Let us speculate good-naturedly about post-biological options. Let's be bold about opening up a broad spectrum of Club-Med post-biological possibilities.

For starters, let's replace the word "death" with the more neutral, precise, scientific term: *Metabolic Coma*. And then let's go on to suggest that this temporary state of "coma" might be replaced by: *Auto-Metamorphosis*, a self-controlled change in bodily form, where the individual chooses to change his/her vehicle of existence without loss of consciousness.

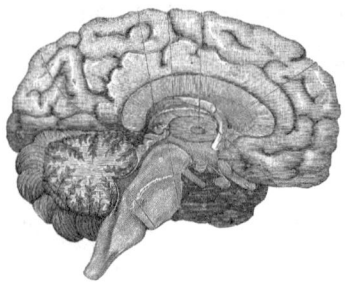

Timothy Leary, Ph.D.,

Then, let's distinguish between involuntary and voluntary metabolic coma. Reversible and irreversible dying.

Let's explore that fascinating "no-man's land"–the period between body-death and neurological-death in terms of the knowledge-information processing involved.

And let's collect some data about that even more intriguing zone now beginning to be researched in the cross-disciplinary field of scientific study known as Artificial Life.[1] What knowledge-information processing capabilities can be preserved after both metabolic coma and brain cessation? What natural and artificial systems, from the growth of mineral structures to the self-reproduction of formal mathematical automata, are promising alternative candidates to biology for the support of life?

And then let us perform the ultimate act of Human Intelligence. Let's venture with calm, open-minded tolerance and

---

[1] Los Alamos, famous as the birthplace of atomic weapons, today also houses the Center for Nonlinear Studies. Several years ago the center sponsored a week long international workshop, the world's first, where scientists met to discuss the implications and craft the foundational theories of the field. The meeting was friendly, fun, and wildly transdisciplinary. Nanotechnology pioneers outlined the potential for protein engineering, and Hans Moravec of the Robotics Institute of Carnegie Mellon University presented compelling arguments that a genetic takeover was underway, our cultural artifacts now evolving past the point of symbiosis with the human species. Self-replicating structures ranging from minerals to computer viruses were demonstrated.

scientific rigor into that perennially mysterious *terra incognita* and ask the final question: What knowledge-information processing possibilities can remain after the cessation of all biological life: somatic, neurological and genetic?

How can human consciousness be supported in hardware outside of the moist envelop of graceful, attractive, pleasure-filled meat we now inhabit? How can the organic, carbon-constructed caterpillar become the silicon butterfly?

C.S. Hyatt, Ph.D. and A.K. O'Shea have suggested three stages of *Post-Biological Intelligence*:

1. *Cybernetic Recognition* of the myriad knowledge-information processing varieties involved in the many stages of dying.

2. *Cybernetic Management*, developing knowledge-information processing skills while out-of-body, out-of-brain, and beyond DNA.

3. *Cybernetic-Technological*, attaining one, or many, of the immortality options.

Post-Biological Recognition Intelligence

We recognize that the dying process, which for millennia has been blanketed by taboo and primitive superstition, has suddenly become accessible to human intelligence.

Here we experience the sudden insights that we need not "go quietly" and passively into the dark night or the neon-lit, Muzak-enhanced Disney-heaven of Christian televangelist's crowd. We realize that the concept of involuntary, irreversible metabolic coma known as death is a feudal superstition, a marketing efficiency of industrial society. We understand that one can discover dozens of active, creative alternatives to going belly-up clutching the company logo of the Christian Cross, Blue Cross, Crescent Cross, or the eligibility cards of the Veterans Administration.

Recognition is always the beginning of the possibility for change. Once we comprehend that "death" can be defined as a problem of knowledge-information processing, solutions to this age-long "problem" can emerge. One realizes the intelligent thing to do is to try to keep one's knowledge-processing capacities around as long as possible. In bodily form. In neural form. In the silicon circuitry and magnetic storage media of today's computers. In molecular form, through the atom stacking of nanotechnology in tomorrow's computers. In cryogenic form. In the form of stored data, legend, myth. In the form of off-spring who are cybernetically trained to use *Post-Biological Intelligence*. In the form of post-biological gene pools, info-pools, advanced viral forms resident in world computer networks and cyberspace matrices of the sort described in the "sprawl novels" of William Gibson.[2]

The second step in attaining *Post-Biological Recognition Intelligence* is to shift from the passive to the active mode. Industrial age humans were trained to await docilely the onset of termination and then to turn over their body for disposal to the priests and the factory (hospital) technicians.

Our species is now developing the Cybernetic Information Skills to plan ahead, to make one's will prevail. The smart thing to do is to see dying as a change in the implementation of information-processing: to orchestrate it, manage it, anticipate and exercise the many available options.

We consider here twenty-two distinct methods of avoiding a submissive or fearful dying.[3]

---

[2] William Gibson, cyberpunk psy-fi visionary, has published *Neuromancer, Count Zero*, and *Burning Chrome*. They are recommended reading for their technically and socially plausible vision of high-tech low-life on the streets.
[3] Mystics may remark that there are also twenty-two paths in the Kabbalistic Tree of Life, associated with the twenty-two cards of the Major Arcana in the Tarot.

Post-Biological Programming Intelligence

Elsewhere the authors have defined eight levels of intelligence: biological emotional, mental-symbolic, social, aesthetic, neurological-cybernetic, genetic, atomic-nanotech. At each stage there is a recognition stage, followed by a brain-programming or brain-reprogramming stage.

In order to reprogram it is necessary to activate the circuits in the brain which mediate that particular dimension of intelligence. Once this circuit is "turned on" it is possible to re-imprint or reprogram.

Cognitive neurology suggests that the most direct way to reprogram emotional responses is to reactivate the appropriate circuits. To reprogram sexual responses it is effective to reactivate and re-experience the original teenage imprints and re-imprint new sexual responses.

The circuits of the brain which mediate the "dying" process are routinely experienced during "near-death" crises. For centuries people have reported: "My entire life flashed before my eyes as I sank for the third time."

This "near-death" experience can be "turned-on" via the relevant anesthetic drugs; ketamine, for example.

Or by learning enough about the effects of out-of-the-body drugs so one can use hypnotic techniques to activate the desired circuits without using external chemical stimuli.

We see immediately the rituals intuitively developed by religious groups are designed to induce trance states related to "dying:' The child growing up in a Catholic culture is deeply imprinted (programmed) by funeral rites. The arrival of the solemn priest to administer extreme unction becomes an access code for the *Post-Biological state*. Other cultures have different rituals for activating and then controlling (programming) the death circuits of the brain. Until recently, very few have permitted personal control or customized consumer choice.

Perhaps this discussion of the "dying circuits of the brain" is too innovative. Sometimes it is easier to understand new concepts about one's own species by referring to other species. Almost every animal species manifests "dying reflexes." Some animals leave the herd to die alone. Others stand with legs apart, stolidly postponing the last moment. Some species eject the dying organism from the social group.

To gain navigational control of one's dying processes three steps suggest themselves: 1) activate the death-reflexes imprinted by your culture, experience them... 2) trace their origins, and... 3) reprogram.

The aim is to develop a scientific model of the chain of cybernetic (knowledge-information) processes that occur as one approaches this metamorphic stage—and to intentionally develop options for taking active responsibility for these events.

Achieving Immortality

Since the dawn of human history, philosophers and theologians have speculated about immortality. Uneasy, aging kings have commanded methods for extending the life span.

A most dramatic example of this age-long impulse is ancient Egypt which produced mummification, the pyramids and manuals like the *Egyptian Book of the Dying*.

The Tibetan Book of the Dead (Buddhist) presents a masterful model of post-mortem stages and techniques for guiding the student to a state of immortality which is neurologically "real" and suggests scientific techniques for reversing the dying process.

The new field of molecular engineering is producing techniques within the framework of current consensus Western Science to implement auto-metamorphosis.

The aim of the game is to defeat death-to give the Individual mastery of this, the final stupidity.

The next section of this essay presents twenty-two methods of achieving immortality. We do not especially endorse any particular technique. Our aim is to review all options and encourage creative-courageous thinking about new possibilities.

A PRELIMINARY LIST OF IMMORTALITY OPTIONS
(To replace Involuntary Irreversible Metabolic Coma)

I. Psychological/Behavioral Training Techniques

The techniques in this category do not assist in attaining personal immortality per se, but are useful in acquiring the experience of "experimental dying;' reversible-voluntary exploration of the territory between body-coma and brain, death, sometimes called out-of-body experiences; or near-dying experiences. Others have termed these astral travel, or reincarnation memories.

1. Meditation and Hypnosis

These are the classic yogic routes to exploration of non-ordinary states of consciousness. They are well known to be labor and time intensive. For the most intelligent and comprehensive discussion of these techniques, we recommend Aleister Crowley.[4]

2. Carefully Designed Psychedelic Drug Experiences of "Dying" and Genetic (Reincarnation/Pre-Incarnation) Consciousness

---

[4] Crowley, Aleister. *Eight Lectures on Yoga*. (Divided into two parts respectively entitled, "Yoga for Yahoos" and "Yoga for Yellowbellies:') New Falcon Publications, 1991.

There is, here, no commitment to any occultist theory about biological incarnation. We refer to techniques enabling access to information and operational programs stored in the brain of the individual. In normal states of consciousness, these are subroutines operating below voluntary access.

3. Experimental Out-of-Body Experiences Using Anesthetics

John Lilly has written extensively about his experiences with small dosages of anesthetics such as ketamine[5]. It is possible that the out-of-body subjective effects of such substances are (merely) interpretations of proprioceptive disruption. Nevertheless, Lilly's reported experiences seem to indicate that information is available through these investigative routes.

4. Sensory Deprivation/Isolation Tanks

Again, Lilly has investigated this subject most comprehensively.

5. Reprogramming Exercises (Suspending the Effects of and Replacing Early "Death" Imprints Imposed by Culture)

6. Development of New Rituals to Guide the Post-Body Transition

Our cultural taboos have prohibited the development of much detailed work in this area. One of the few available sources in this area is E. J. Gold.[6]

7. Pre-Incarnation Exercises

With these, one uses the preferred altered state method (drugs, hypnosis, shamanic trance, voodoo ritual, born-again frenzies) to create future scripts for oneself.

---

[5] Walford, Roy L., M.D. *The 120 Year Diet*. Simon & Schuster, 1986. Norton, W. W. *Maximum Life Span*. New York, 1983.
[6] Gold, E. J. *American Book of the Dead*. IDHHB, 1973. See also Gold's *Creation Story Verbatim*.

8. *Aesthetically-Orchestrated Voluntary "Dying"*
This procedure has been called suicide, i.e., "self-murder;' by officials who wish to control the mortem process. Mr. and Mrs. Arthur Koestler, active members of the British EXIT program arranged a most dignified and graceful voluntary metabolic coma. A California group, HADDA, is placing an amendment on California ballot to permit terminal patients to plan voluntary metacom with their medical advisors.

The non-Californian can always look for an enlightened M.D., or consenting adult friends to act as guides to the Western Lands.

II. Somatic Techniques for Life Extension

Techniques to inhibit the process of aging comprise the classical approach to immortality. In the present state of science these "buy time."

9. *Diet*
The classic research on diet and longevity has been performed by Roy L. Walford, M.D.[7]

10. *Life-Extension Drugs*
These include antioxidants and others. A comprehensive reference is *Life Extension* by Sandy Shaw and Durk Pearson.

11. *Exercise Regimes*

12. *Temperature Variation*

13. *Sleep Treatments (Hibernation)*

14. *Immunization to Counter the Aging Process*

---

[7] Walford, Roy L., M.D. The 120 Year Diet. Simon & Schuster, 1986. Norton, W. W. Maximum Life Span. New York, 1983.

III. Somatic/Neural/Genetic Preservation

Techniques in this class do not ensure continuous operation of consciousness. They produce potentially reversible metabolic coma. They are alternatives for preserving the structure of tissues until a time of more advanced medical knowledge.

15. Cryogenics or Vacuum-Pack "Pickling"

Why let one's body and brain rot when that seems to imply no possibility at all for your future? Why let the carefully arranged tangle of dendritic growths in your nervous system which may be the storage site for all of your memories get eaten by fungus? Perpetual preservation of your tissues is available today at moderate cost.[8]

16. Cryonic Preservation of Neural Tissue or DNA

Those not particularly attached to their bodies can opt for preservation of the essentials: their brains together with the instructional codes capable of re-growing something genetically identical to their present bio-machinery.

IV. Bio-Genetic Methods for Life Extension

Is there any need to experience metabolic coma at all? We have mentioned ways to gain personal control of the experience, to stave it off by "conventional" longevity techniques, to avoid irreversible dissolution of the systemic substrate.

Techniques are now emerging to permit a much more vivid guarantee of personal persistence, a smooth metamorphic transformation into a different form of substrate on which the computer program of consciousness runs.

---

[8] One of the few cryogenic preservation companies in operation is the Alcor Foundation.

17. Cellular/DNA Repair

Nanotechnology is the science and engineering of mechanical and electronic systems built at atomic dimensions.[9] One forecast ability of nanotechnology is its potential for production of self-replicating nano-machines living within individual biological cells.

These artificial enzymes will effect cellular repair, as damage occurs from mechanical causes, radiation, or other aging effects. Repair of DNA ensures genetic stability.

18. Cloning

Biologically-based replication of genetically identical personal copies of yourself, at any time desired, is approaching the possible. Sex is fun, but sexual reproduction is biologically inefficient, suited mainly for inducing genetic variation in species which still advance through the accidents of luck in random combination.

---

[9] The most visible and eloquent proponent of nanotechnology is K. Eric Drexler of MIT and Stanford Universities. His book *Engines of Creation* provides a detailed overview of the held. Other more technical works include:

Drexler, K. Eric. "Molecular Engineering: An Approach to the Development of General Capabilities for Molecular Manipulation." Proc. Natl. Acad. Sci USA, Vol. 78, No. 9, September 1981, pp. 5275-5278.

Drexler, K. Eric. "Rod Logic & Thermal Noise in the Mechanical Nanocomputer." Proc. Third Intl. Symposium on Molecular Electronic Devices, Elsevier North Holland, 1987.

Drexler, K. Eric. "Molecular Engineering: Assemblers and Future Space Hardware:' Aerospace XXI, thirty-third annual meeting of the American Astronomical Society, Paper AAS-86-415.

Feynman, Richard. "There's Plenty of Room at the Bottom." Speech transcript in *Miniaturization*. Gilbert, H. D. (ed.), Reinhold, New York, 1961, pp. 282-296. One of the original works approaching molecular-scale engineering. Nobel Prize-winner Feynman is without a doubt one of the most brilliant scientists of his century.

V. Cybernetic (Post-Biological) Methods for Attaining Immortality [Artificial Life in Silicon]

As the neuromantic cyberpunk author Bruce Sterling notes, evolution moves in clades, radiating outward in omnidirectional diversity, and not following a single linear path. Some silicon visionaries believe that natural evolution of the human species (or at least their branch of it) is near completion. They are no longer interested in merely procreating, but in designing their successors. Carnegie Mellon robot scientist Hans Moravec said, "We owe our existence to organic evolution. But we owe it little loyalty. We are on the threshold of a change in the universe comparable to the transition from non-life, to life."[10]

Human society has now reached a turning point in the operation of the process of evolution, a point at which the next evolutionary step of the species is under our control. Or, more correctly, the next steps, which will occur in parallel, will result in an explosion of diversity of the human species. We are no longer dependent on fitness in any physical sense for survival, our quantum appliances and older mechanical devices provide the requisite means in all circumstances. In the near future, the (now merging) methods of computer and biological technology will make the human form a matter totally determined by individual choice.

As a flesh and blood species we are moribund, stuck at "a local optimum;' to borrow a term from mathematical optimization theory.

Beyond this horizon, which humankind has reached, lies the unknown, the as-yet scarcely imagined. We will design

---

[10] Moravec, Hans. Mind Children: The Future of Robot and Human Intelligence. Harvard University Press, 1988.

our children, and co-evolve intentionally with the cultural artifacts which are our progeny.

Humans already come in some variety of races and sizes. In comparison to what "human" will mean within the next century, we humans are at present as indistinguishable from one another as are hydrogen molecules. Our anthropocentrism will decrease.

We see two principle categorizations of the form of the human of the future, one more biological-like: a bio/machine hybrid of any desired form, and one not biological at all: an "electronic life" on the computer networks. Human-as machine, and human-in-machine.

Of these, human-as-machine is perhaps more easily conceived. Today, we already have crude prosthetic implants, artificial limbs, valves, and entire organs. The continuing improvements in old-style mechanical technology slowly increase the thoroughness of human-machine integration.

The electronic life form of human-in-machine is even more alien to our current conceptions of humanity. Through storage of one's belief systems as on-line data structures, driven by selected control structures (the electronic analog to will?), one's neuronal apparatus will operate in silicon as it did on the wetware of the brain, although faster, more accurately, more self-mutably, and, if desired, immortally.

19. Archival-Informational

One standard way of becoming "immortal" is by leaving a trail of archives, biographies, and publicized noble deed.

The increasing presence of stable knowledge media in our Cybernetic Society make this a more rigorous platform for persistent existence. The knowledge possessed by an individual is captured in expert systems, and world-scale hyper-text systems[11] thus ensuring the longevity and accessibility of textural and graphical memes.

Viewed from outside the self, death is not a binary phenomenon, but a continuously varying function. How alive are you in Paris at this moment? In the city in which you live? In the room in which you are reading this?

20. Head Coach Personality Database Transmission

Head Coach was a computer system once under development by Futique, Inc.[12], one of the first examples of psychoactive computer software. The program would have allowed the user (performer) to digitize and store thoughts on a routine daily basis. If one leaves, let us say, twenty years of daily computer-stored records of thought-performance, one's grandchildren a century down the line could have "known" and replayed your information habits and mental performances. They would have been able to "share and relive experiences" in considerable detail. To take a most vulgar example, if an individual's moves in a chess game are stored, the descendants can relive, move-by-move, a game played by their great-great-grandmother in the past century.

---

[11] A world-scale hypertext system to permit instantaneous on-line access to global knowledge networks has been envisioned and written about by Ted Nelson in *Literary Machine*, published by the author. Other information is available in Nelson's *Computer Lib*, published in 1974 and republished in 1987 by Microsoft Press.

[12] Timothy Leary coined the term "futique;' which he said is the opposite of antique, when he began designing computer software in the 1980s. Futique was a consortium of artists, writers, programmers, designers, educators, and philosophers all working toward a common goal. When Leary was near the end of (t)his life, he put all his assets IN TRUST for the future-and so Futique, Inc. is now known as The Futique Trust. The trust is principally his archival material which consists of a huge collection of papers and memorabilia from his birth certificate, through all phases of his life and his attention-getting death in 1996. (www.timothylearyarchives.org/futique-trust)

As passive reading is replaced by "active rewriting;" later generations would have been able to relive how we performed the great books of our time.

Yet more intriguing is the possibility of implementing the knowledge extracted over time from a person: their beliefs, preferences, and tendencies, as a set of algorithms guiding a program capable of acting in a manner functionally identical to the person. Advances in robotics technology will take these "turing creatures" away from being mere "brains in bottles" to hybrids capable of interacting sensorially with the physical world.

21. Nanotech Information Storage: Towards Direct Brain-Computer Transfer

When a computer becomes obsolete, one does not discard the data it contains. The hardware is merely a temporary vehicle of implementation for structures of information. The data gets transferred to new systems for continued use. Decreasing costs of computer storage, CD-ROM and WORM memory systems, mean that no information generated today ever need be lost.

We can consider building an artificial computational substrate both functionally and structurally identical to the brain (and perhaps the body). How? Via the predicted future capabilities of nanotechnology.[13]

Communicating nano-machines which pervade the organism may analyze the neural and cellular structure and transfer the information obtained to machinery capable of growing, atom by atom, an identical copy.

---

[13] We partially regret such speculations beyond present technical capabilities. The brain is a most complex machine, with some 10^{20} individual cells, according to some estimates. Yet we are redeemed by what we see as the technical inevitability of nanotechnology.

But what of the soul? According to the *American Heritage Dictionary*, "soul [is] the animating and vital principle in man credited with the faculties of thought, action and emotion and conceived as forming an immaterial entity distinguishable from but temporarily coexistent with his body."

At first reading this definition seems to be a classic example of theological nonsense. But studied from the perspective of information theory we may be able to wrestle this religio-babble into scientific operations. Let's change the bizarre word "immaterial" to "invisible to the naked senses" i.e., atomic/molecular/electronic. Now the "soul" refers to information processed and stored in microscopic-cellular, molecular packages. Soul becomes any information that "lives;' i.e., is capable of being retrieved and communicated. Is it not true that all the tests for "death" at every level of measurement (nuclear, neural, bodily, galactic) involve checking for unresponsiveness to signals?

From this viewpoint, the twenty-two immortality options become cybernetic methods of preserving one's unique signal capacity. There are as many souls as there are ways storing and communicating data. Tribal lore defines the racial soul. The DNA is a molecular soul. The brain is a neurological soul. Electron storage creates the silicon soul. Nanotechnology makes possible the atomic soul.

22. Computer Viral: Persistent Existence in Gibson's Cyberspace Matrix

The previous option permitted personal survival through isomorphic mapping of neural structure to silicon (or some other arbitrary medium of implementation). It also suggests the possibility of survival as an entity in what amounts to a reification of Jung's collective unconscious: the global information network.

In a fictitious twenty-first century imagined by William Gibson, wily cybernauts will not only store themselves electronically, but do so in the form of a "computer virus;' capable of traversing computer networks and of self-replication as a guard against accidental or malicious erasure by others, or other programs. (Imagine the somewhat droll scenario: "What's on this CD?" "Ah, that's just old Leary. Let's go ahead and reformat it.")

Given the ease of copying computer-stored information, one could exist simultaneously in many forms. Where the "I" is in this situation is a matter for philosophy. Our belief is that consciousness would persist in each form, running independently (and ignorant of each other self-manifestation unless in communication with it), cloned at each branch point.

[NOTE: This list of options for Voluntary-Reversible-Metabolic Coma and auto-metamorphosis is not mutually exclusive. The intelligent person needs little encouragement to explore all of these possibilities. And to design many new other alternatives to going belly-up in line with Management Memos.]

Kon-Tiki of the Flesh

In the near future, what is now taken for granted as the perishable human creature will be a mere historical curiosity, one point amidst unimaginable multidimensional diversity of form. Individuals, or groups of adventurers, will be free to choose to reassume flesh-and-blood form, constructed for the occasion by the appropriate science.

Such historical expeditions may well be conducted in the spirit of Thor Heyerdahl's Kon-Tiki voyages. To voyage in what the light of history reveals to be an objectively improbable way, merely to prove that such was possible, as unlikely as it seems.

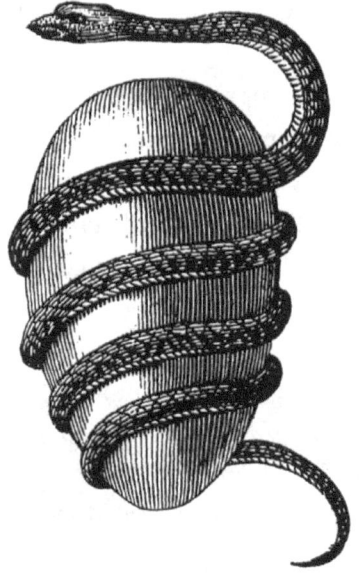

THEURGIA LIBERATIO: MAGIC AS DIVINE LIBERATION
Chic & S. Tabatha Cicero

> *"The technique of Magic is one by which the soul flies, straight as an arrow impelled from a taut bow, to serenity, to a profound and impenetrable repose. But it is only man himself who may tauten the string of the bow; none else may accomplish this task for him."*
>
> -Israel Regardie
> from *The Tree of Life: An Illustrated Study in Magic*

To modern society at large, the subject of magic is one of those hot-button topics that tends to trigger widely differing emotional reactions. Most people undoubtedly believe individuals who practice magic are primitive, superstitious, crazy, or all three. Another segment of the population, specifically religious fundamentalists, believe ALL magic is an evil practice performed by people who, if not evil themselves, are nonetheless the dupes of evil-those who are tricked into performing their unholy rites by the deceptive encouragement of "THE DEVIL" (Cue ominous music!)

Magic is often described in terms are both scientific and religious, to the consternation of both scientists and clergy. It has been defined as "the method of science, the aim of religion." It is precisely because magic encroaches on the territories of both that it often receives the slings and arrows of the egocentric scientist and the resentful cleric. Of these two groups, however, the criticism originating from the indignant clergy is the more shrill, hateful, and uniformed. Yet magic is only one of the more recent recipients of these attacks. Not long ago the science of mathematics was considered a form of sorcery, and mathematicians were viewed with suspicion.

What is it about the practice of magic that makes fundamentalists condemn it so?

Beyond the obvious fact that humans often denounce what they do not understand, there is also the undisputed fact that magical practice flies directly in the face of the fundamentalist's agenda: to proselytize, to convert, and to persuade as many people as possible to think the same way, pray the same prayers, worship the same deity, attend the same churches, listen to the same pastors, and fill the same coffers. For centuries, Western theocrats have based their agenda on Constantine's fourth century approach: One Emperor, One Empire, One God, One Religion. One unified bureaucracy ruling it all. One particular set of Christian beliefs was exalted and all others condemned. Deviation was discouraged, to put it mildly. Other forms of worship were exiled, died out, or went underground. This was the religious reality of the West for centuries until cracks started to appear in the theological door, nailed into place by Luther's hammer.

New Christian sects soon flourished, but most also embraced Constantine's approach-there was one right set of beliefs and all others were wrong. Each sect taught that it alone had the One True Way, and all other sects were deceived, blinkered, misinformed, or bound for hell. Adherents were taught that following the instructions of the church (whichever sect it happened to be) would result in happiness and salvation. Following a different church could result in damnation and eternal misery. Such was the kindling that sparked religious conflicts such as the Thirty Years War and the Inquisition.

With the Renaissance came a resurgence in classical knowledge and philosophy. The Age of Reason (seventeenth century) and the Age of Enlightenment (eighteenth century) followed and built on the scientific advancements of preceding ages. In ways never been previously possible, more and more people began to examine their deepest-held beliefs concerning God, religion, and humanity's relationship to the Divine. Influential thinkers of the day began an intellectual revolution against the yoke of religious orthodoxy-sometimes quietly, sometimes vociferously. As evidenced by such documents as Pope Leo XIII's "Human Genus: Against Freemasonry and Spirit of the Age" (1884), which condemned such ideas as "democracy"–power over individual human lives gradually slipped away from church, which kicked and screamed at every lost bit of control and authority.

It was against this backdrop that the nineteenth century "Occult Revival" was born, ushering in a proliferation of esoteric societies and such thinkers as Eliphas Levi, Helena Blavatsky, W. Wynn Westcott, S. L. MacGregor Mathers, Aleister Crowley, Arthur Edward Waite, and others. At the heart of this revival was the study of magic; a yearning for liberation of the human spirit through arcane knowledge.

THE LIBERATING PROPERTIES OF MAGIC

The magic of the West is often described as hermetic, named for an ancient magician known as Hermes Trismegistus, the legendary author of several books on the occult sciences, whose name is in turn derived from the messenger god Hermes. One of the principle aims of magic is the

1. Arthur Edward Waite 2. S.L. MacGregor Mathers
3. W. Wynn Westcott   4. Helena Blavatsky

elevation/ evolution of the human psyche to its highest potential. For some this may allude to an inner communication with a subjective part of the self, often called the Higher Self, the Soul, or the Higher and Divine Genius. Others take this to mean a more objective state of communication and guidance under the name of Holy Guardian Angel, Daemon, or "inner planes contact." The methods used to facilitate this communication include the study and performance of various occult sciences grouped together under the banner of magic.

Magic is the art and science of causing change to occur in conformity with will. This change can occur: 1) in the outer, manifest world, 2) in the magician's consciousness, and 3) most often in both, for changing one often changes the other. Magical change occurs in a way that is not currently understood by modern science because it works through the Unmanifest through subtle manipulations of the invisible, spiritual realms. However, the workings of magic are subject to natural law. The effects of magic are sometimes clearly visible in the physical world, but other times they are only apparent on a personal, spiritual level. The workings of magic are not limited by the constraints of time and space.

Magic is liberated from the current conventions of material science, although science may someday understand how and why magic works. Magic is also liberated from the concepts of time and space, because the astral realms where magic works are constrained by neither.

In ancient times magic and religion were regarded as one and the same: they shared a fundamental origin and unity. However, modern magic, which can be considered a refinement of "medieval magic" is entirely distinct from religion-it is *technique* as opposed to belief. The separation of magic from religion in the West occurred primarily because of the prohibition against magic by a domineering church. But it also resulted partly from a truce that Renaissance humanists were forced to make with religious leaders–namely, that the church was the sole authority on the Divine and the heavenly powers, while the natural (mundane) world, including the celestial spheres and the elements, fell under the purview of the scientist and the philosopher. Esoteric thinkers such as Marsilio Ficino had to maintain that magical workings involved purely natural forces that did not infringe upon the domain claimed by the church. This unsteady cease fire was successful for a brief time until rebellious humanists such as Pico della Mirandola pushed the envelope with the study of Qabalah and its myriad of angels, archangels and divine emanations-all of which magicians use effect change.

Methods of magic include invocation, evocation, divination, the creation and consecration of talismans, skrying and other forms of astral work, vibration, meditation, visualization, and ceremonial ritual. Magic has its own set of attributes, mental processes, and natural laws, whereas religion depends more on faith, creed, and official doctrine. In short, religion is a *specific belief* or set of beliefs, values, and practices usually based on the teachings of a spiritual leader. Magic is a *method or mechanism* of causing change to occur in the material world in accordance with cosmic laws. In a very simplified analogy, magic inclines toward *thinking and doing* while religion gravitates toward *feeling and being*. The two are very definitely related, but they are not identical. The yearning for the supernatural propels them both, though in different ways.

Organized religion tends to limit access to the supernatural world within the bulwark of a formalized theology, and the faithful are strongly encouraged to remain within that framework. In magic, however, the individual is encouraged to experience the supernatural realms for him or herself. While religion often focuses on the group experience, group-think and group interdependence, usually with a single religious leader or small group of leaders shepherding their flock, magic emphasizes the individual experience, independent thought, and belief that is based on personal revelation of the Divine. These are qualities that the magic shares with mysticism.

In her book *Practical Occultism* Evelyn Underhill described mysticism as "... the art of union with Reality. The mystic is a person who has attained that union in greater or less degree; or who aims at and believes in such attainment." This goal is no less than the Completion of the Great Work espoused by magicians. The primary methods used by mystics are prayer, devotion, meditation, and contemplation. However, mystics such as Underhill have been known to be every bit as unsympathetic toward magic as are orthodox clergy. Concerning these esoteric sibling rivalries, Dion Fortune set the record straight in her book *Esoteric Orders and Their Work* by comparing the mystic and the magician,

> It is amusing to note that, while the occultist decries the spiritualist, the mystic looks askance at the occultist; yet a mystic is simply an introvert occultist, and the occultist an extrovert mystic. Both aim at the same goal, though they seek it by different methods. The difference between them is of temperament, not of ideal. When the scientific temperament approaches the Unseen, it chooses to Occult Path of development, and when the artistic temperament approaches the Unseen, it chooses the Mystic Path; one progresses through right knowing and the other through right feeling, and both meet in the end. Difference of method should never blind us to unity of aim.
> The mystic pursues a solitary path, even when he is a member of a community; his visions are for himself alone, and he has often but little power to teach that which he has himself learnt. He reaches the heights of the spirit and dwells there apart; his experience is a personal one, and cannot be communicated to others. He is essentially the artistic temperament working upon the things of the spirit; creative, joyous, and inspiring to those who can appreciate his art because they are akin to him in nature. Esotericism, without a touch of mystic rapture, would be as drab as a culture that had no place for the beautiful; but a spiritual culture which is purely mystical has little

relation to the problems of humanity and no message for the common man.

Occultism, on the other hand, is of the intellect. The occult path is followed in cooperation with others, because its heights are achieved by means of group-work and the use of ritual.

While mysticism represents a passive path, magic is the active path of spiritual liberation. It is often called theurgy or "God-working" because the magician is an active participant in his or her own quest to approach the Light of the Divine and the profound peace of illumination. What is certain is while many true, sincere mystics are not magicians, many true, sincere magicians are also mystics.

THE PSYCHOLOGICAL LIBERATION OF MAGIC

In addition to its spiritual qualities, there is another useful property of magic-theurgy as a tool for psychological liberation. Israel Regardie, in *The Middle Pillar: The Balance Between Mind and Body*, compared the sublimating effects of magical work to the healing of the mind/psyche garnered by psychotherapy,

> Analytical psychology and magic comprise in my estimation two halves or aspects of a single technical system. Just as the body and mind are not two separate units, but are simply the dual manifestations of an interior dynamic 'something; so psychology and magic comprise similarly a single system whose goal in the integration of the human personality. Its aim is to unify the different departments and functions of man's being, to bring into operation those which previously for various reasons were latent. Incidentally, its technique is such that neurotic symptoms which were too insistent upon expression either become illuminated or toned down by a process of equilibration.

The goal of both magic and psychotherapy is the growth and well being of the individual on every level-physical, mental, and psychological. But one element is missing from modern psychology–the spiritual essence of humanity and divine character of life. Theurgy includes what psychology had long forgotten–the spiritual welfare of the individual.

Inner alchemy is another field closely related to our discussion. The alchemist works to separate, purify, and recombine the principle components of whatever substance being worked with-whether the object of his work is a base metal, an organic substance, or their own human soul. The fundamental objective is integration, or the liberation of the base material from the limitations (and illusions) of separateness, a goal alchemy shares with both psychotherapy and magic. All three fields can be said to involve three similar stages of progression. In alchemy these stages are called separation, purification, and cohobation (recombination). In psychology they are referred to as analysis, confrontation (of the shadow), and individuation (self-realization). In magic these stages are often called purification, consecration, and union (with the Higher Self). All are simply different terms for the same essential experience: liberation of one's highest human potential. However, the sacerdotal art of magic is the most direct and inspired.

As is often the case, no author is more eloquent on the subject than Israel Regardie, who says in his book Foundations of *Practical Magic: An Introduction to Qabalistic, Magical and Meditative Techniques*,

> [Magic] deals with that sphere of the psyche of which normally we are not conscious but which exerts an enormous influence upon our lives. Magic is a series of psychological techniques so devised as to enable us to probe

Dr. Israel Regardie
Painting by Delfina Marquez-Noe

more deeply into ourselves. To what end? First, that we shall understand ourselves more completely. Apart from the fact that such self-knowledge in itself is desirable, an understanding of the inner nature releases us from unconscious compulsions and motivations and confers a mastery over life. Second, that we may the more fully express that inner self in everyday activities. It is only when men and women have reached, or perhaps when the more advanced men and women in the world have evolved, some degree of inner realization that we may ever hope for that ideal utopian condition of things–a wide tolerance, peace, and universal brotherhood. It is to such as these that Magic owes its *raison d'etre*.

INITIATION: A NEW BEGINNING

For those who seek to actively work with those of a like mind, initiation is the preliminary step into the realm of magic. From ancient times up to the present today, initiation ceremonies have played a major role in mystery traditions and magical groups. Spiritual seekers of the past were drawn to the rites of Isis and Osiris, Eleusis, Samothrace, and Orpheus because of the sense of spiritual vigor and euphoria they provided through elaborate initiation ceremonies.

The word initiation means "to begin." Magical initiation into a specific magical group represents the passage into a distinctly esoteric mind-set and spiritual outlook. The Western Magical Tradition encompasses many branches of the Hermetic Tree–Khemetic, Hellenic, Gnostic, Neo-Platonic, Qabalistic, Alchemical, Rosicrucian, Golden Dawn, Thelemic, Ogdoadic, etc. Teaching organizations and mystery schools can be found for all of these respective paths.

The advantages of group work are many. Mystery schools past and present were founded by individuals motivated by any number of reasons, but the best are usually inspired to teacher, whether by inner planes contacts or divine muse, to offer a useful curriculum of esoteric work that can guide the student step-by-step through the magical/alchemical process of purification, consecration, and union. To be an Initiate means one is accepted into an inner circle whose teachings and rituals are meaningful only to other members of the group who share this common experience. According to Dion Fortune, "Students of esoteric science have always tended to band themselves together into caravans for the purpose of taking the Golden Journey." Admittance to such a group confers a sense of fellowship and belonging, of receiving arcane information, and of having been uplifted through the disclosure of divinely inspired wisdom. "The occultist goes by a well-marked way which has been trodden by countless feet from time immoral:' This does not mean the would-be spiritual rebel simply trades in one congregation for another. A magical order is not a religion and is not designed to take the place of religion, although religious symbolism is often used in ceremonies as a catalyst to stimulate the alchemical process of self-evolution. The rite of initiation is meant to purify the candidate and prepare him or her to receive the teachings of the group, which can aid and support one's personal process of illumination. Ultimately, however, the Initiate is in control of his or her own destiny. Spiritual attainment within a magical group still depends on the individual will, perseverance, merits, and character of the student.

MAGICAL INITIATION: FOUR PITFALLS TO AVOID

Magicians often describe the wonderful experiences they have had during initiation or as a result of initiation into the mysteries. For most, initiations are deeply inspiring, meaningful, and even cathartic experiences. However, as in all things, there can be a downside to magical initiation. In his article "The Darker Side of Initiation," Donald Michael Kraig listed four dangers the student should be aware of when seeking out initiation into any magical group: failure, fakes, abuse, and self-deception. These four pitfalls threaten the spiritual liberation the student is searching for. Here we will examine each of these hazards in turn.

1. Failure: Liberation Short-Circuited

A large proportion of people who join magical groups will never make it all the way through the grade system of whatever group they have joined. This is a true, simple fact. Most leaders of magical groups will tell you the percentage of people who persevere and continue on to work the highest grades of their respective system is less than ten percent; sometimes much less.

We are certainly not saying that who leaves a particular magical group is "blowing" their chance at spiritual liberation. True magical liberation is personal and can only come from within–it is not dependant on any group. There are many good reasons students leave magical groups: health reasons, distance issues, family obligations, work-related time constraints, changes in one's religious outlook, spiritual path changes, etc. A student may leave a specific magical group and find another that is more suitable to his or her spiritual needs. We are not talking about that here.

Liberation short-circuited is failure to launch. Some people leave a magical group because of their own faulty expectations of what magic, initiation, or group work entails. Students drop out only to denounce that the group had any value whatsoever, sometimes writing off magic entirely. Some go so far as to condemn what they were previously involved in. In cases such as this, the ex-student does not recognize that the true failure was either in his or her own lack of authentic, inner initiation or their own misunderstanding of the experience. They also falsely assume because the magic did not work for them, it will not work for anybody else.

One example of this was a student who left our Order shortly after receiving a Neophyte initiation, because she had expected to see and experience the hand of God literally reaching down and embracing her during the initiation. She was very disappointed when the hand did not appear! Failure to Launch.

Another example was a student who wanted to invoke Enochian entities while he was still in the Outer Order, against our advice. (While some Outer Order students may be magically advanced enough to do this, we were certain this particular student was not.) This was a classic case of "lust for results" or performing complex magical workings just to "see what happens." In nearly every case of this kind, students involved don't really believe that magic is real, and so they perform advanced theurgical workings they are not ready for, precisely because they want to experience the kind of magical "special effects" seen in Hollywood movies about the occult. In our example, the student in question was frightened when he opened psychological doors he was totally unprepared to deal with. He dropped out of the Order and swore off magic entirely.

The end result of magical failure to launch is a feeling of general negativity, pessimism, and possibly depression that can last for quite a long time.

2. Fakes: Liberation Mislead

Fraternal organizations and magical groups have a long tradition of tracing their hereditary roots back to the esoteric societies and archaic religions of earlier times–to the sixteenth century Rosicrucians, the medieval Knights Templar, the ancient Israelites, the Egyptians, the Babylonians, and even the inhabitants of Atlantis, lost in the mists of time. While these various legends of ancient initiatory lineages can provide inspiration, allegorical drama, and symbolic knowledge that can be of great value to the Initiate, they almost always breakdown under the scrutiny of historical fact.

For several decades (if not centuries) wild claims made by esoteric leaders, fraternities, and magical groups of all stripes have misled countless spiritual seekers. Fake lineages, claims of unique apostolic succession, and outrageous assertions of superhuman powers have become so common among magical groups vying for members that the image of the charlatan magician or con artist guru is almost a proverb.

The founders of the Golden Dawn were not guilt free in this respect, since most reputable Golden Dawn scholars have concluded that Westcott's continental contact "Fraulein

Sprengel" was invented to give the fledging Order a proper pedigree for its era. We can absolve Westcott's sin because we believe the end result–the creation of the Golden Dawn was positive and useful.

What is far less forgivable is the repetition of such creation myths by modern day myth makers who fabricate a magical apostolic succession stretching back nearly to the prehistoric age. These are the magicians and groups who wear their empty claims of superiority on their sleeve and boast of having an impressive lineage or charter they never show to anyone, lest they be discovered to be the frauds that they are. As far as spiritual teachers go, these are generally the ones who publicly claim Christ-like piety while privately behaving like frat boys gone wild.

If this sounds like an unfair critique of those who pad their magical resumes in order to dupe their followers, it is certainly not the first of its kind. We can turn to many of the great esoteric thinkers of the past to hear harsher assessments. In *Esoteric Orders and Their Work*, Dion Fortune warned "Such groups are innumerable at the present time, and may either represent the door ajar, or a snare and a delusion..." William Gray, author of *Inner Traditions of Magic,* advised seekers to,

> ...be highly suspicious of all demands for money or pretentious claims made on material levels... It is best to avoid commercialism in any form of disguise if genuine spiritual development is sought. No matter what chicanery is used to camouflage money-motive and power policies, they remain today what they always were, traps that lead Light seekers into confusion and disorders of the worst kind...

In *Words of Wisdom*, Manly P. Hall offers one of the most cutting indictments of all, calling them "metaphysical carpetbaggers who are indeed parasites which have attached themselves to the tree of philosophy." Hall tells us that "the fraudulent metaphysician is usually finally convicted by his own words and actions," and that his misrepresentations usually fall into a few easily detected categories,

> He is generally the only possessor of some very superlative truth which he has received direct from... some equally august source difficult to check on... He is willing to communicate this extraordinary knowledge to anyone who has... dollars, in ten easy lessons which inevitably lead to adeptship... He nearly always implies that possession of the peculiar knowledge of which he is the sole owner (copyright applied for) will inevitably cause the individual fortunate enough to receive his instruction to become healthy, wealthy, and wise...

Would such "peculiar knowledge" and questionable lineage be valuable to one's magical liberation if it karmically linked the student to a teacher whose words and actions run completely opposite to the ideals, principles, and ethics he or she claims to uphold? Unfortunately, the second pitfall of magical initiation *(liberation mislead)*, often goes hand-in-hand with the next hazard-abuse.

3. Abuse: Liberation vs. Enslavement

The practice of magic is an important avenue for personal liberation and spiritual evolution. How ironic is it then, that when prospective students attempt to seek out legitimate schools of magic they sometimes run the risk of entangling themselves with a group that is not so much "occult" as it is "a cult?" What about teachers or groups that claim to instruct students in the liberating techniques of magic, and then proceed to drain students' bank accounts, interfere with their personal lives, demand absolute obedience, or take over their free will?

In such scenarios the rational for magic gets turned on its head–liberation is transformed into enslavement; the enslavement of naive seekers by unscrupulous gurus and abusive "spiritual leaders." How does the aspiring magical "rebel" avoid being duped into becoming just another compliant sheep in a submissive herd, waiting to get fleeced?

This is no new problem. More than a century ago, Dion Fortune warned readers to stay clear of dodgy groups and teachers. She advised students to look for three things in a reputable teacher: right principles, genuine knowledge, and "such common sense and capacity as shall prevent a teacher from involving his pupils in muddles and misadventures." Fortune goes on to say,

> ... for all practical purposes the neophyte is pretty much in the hands of his initiator at the outset, and if the senior occultist's power is abused, the neophyte is in for an unpleasant experience, to say the least of it. The true initiator will no more exercise undue influence over his pupil nor abuse his superior knowledge than will the honourable doctor over his patient nor the honourable lawyer over his client; but there are black sheep in every profession, and the occult world; unfortunately, is not sufficiently organized to permit of its black sheep being officially deprived of their power to practise. Therefore the would-be pupil has to look to himself pretty sharply, especially in his early days before he knows the ropes.

Abuse in occult circles usually starts with unreasonable demands for unquestioning obedience to a single leader. Again, the original Golden Dawn was not blameless in this regard: S. L. MacGregor Mathers made such a demand of the London Adepts, going so far as to expel one member, Annie Horniman, even after she submitted to his demands. (This event, as much as any other, helped to sow the seeds of discord, which finally led to the Order's break-up in 1903. It was also a bone-headed move since Horniman was Mathers' financial benefactor. Shortly after he expelled her, Mathers and his wife asked Horniman for more money!)

It is essential students be able to discern the difference between a legitimate group that will foster the Candidate's spiritual growth and one that exists primarily to benefit the leader(s) of the group. Students should steer well clear of groups that exploit students in terms of money, power, sexual gratification, etc.

Abusive behavior in esoteric groups can be relatively harmless, as was the case with S. L. MacGregor Mathers' demands (the main result of which was the implosion of the Order), or it can be harmful in the extreme. The poster child for everything that can go horribly wrong in such a group was the Order of the Solar Temple, a doomsday cult responsible for the deaths of seventy-four of its followers in Quebec, Switzerland, and France between 1994 and 1997.

The only way for the student to know for certain whether a group is sincere or abusive is to ask specific questions of people in the wider esoteric community. Questions such as: Does the group exhibit excessive devotion or fanatical dedication to some person, idea, or goal? Does it use manipulative techniques of persuasion and control? Do the group's leaders encourage isolation from family and friends? Do group leaders actively promote the break-up of relationships? Does the organization exert powerful group pressures, information management, and other methods to suspend the individual's critical judgment? Do the leaders of the organization promote complete dependency on the group and the fear or consequences of leaving it? Do the leaders demand subservience or an unreasonable amount of work to be done for "the good of the group?" Does the goal of the group seem designed to benefit the group's leaders to the actual or possible detriment of members? Do the leaders of the group continually ask members for money or donations? Do the leaders of the group regularly engage in acts of harmful magic and/or smear campaigns against others, or encourage their members to engage in such acts? Does the leader make unreasonable demands for absolute obedience from his or her students? Vigilant students can save themselves years of stress, disappointment, and heartache by finding out the answers to these important questions. According to Dion Fortune there is also the option of self-initiation, which is always open to the student of the Mysteries,

> The solitary worker, depending on aspiration and meditation; and unguided save by his intuition, although his progress may be slower, is in a much better position than the blind follower of a blind leader.
> Remember that it is always better to be alone than in bad company, and that you need never fear that your occult progress will be retarded by a sacrifice made on the altar of principle.

4. Self-Deception: Liberation Unrecognized

The final hazard to be avoided is self-deception, which can be the most subtle and difficult challenge of all. Self-deception can take many forms; from the student who takes an initiation and thinks that he or she instantly gains great psychic or magical powers, to the teacher whose ego expands to messianic proportions. People who are natural clairvoyants and mediums are especially susceptible, as are those with chemical imbalances or other psychological problems. As ironic as it sounds, a healthy dose of skepticism is required to safely traverse the astral planes where magic is worked. Magicians must be scientists of the mind-testing every visionary experience for kernels of truth and husks of delusion. Without taking the proper precautions it becomes far too easy for some to lose their way in the ethereal realms. They run the risk of becoming "astral junkies" unable to distinguish divine revelation from flights of fantasy-spiritual breakthrough from psychic breakdown.

The practice of magic works to release latent energy from the subconscious and expand the mind's horizons. As the magician becomes proficient in the theurgical arts he or she undergoes an increase in psychic awareness, knowledge, and self-confidence. This is often accompanied by feelings of new life-purpose and direction. But magic can also sometimes reawaken the mechanism of the infantile mega-ego, causing delusions of grandeur and self-importance. In this case, the rebel simply becomes a slave to a new Master: the all-consuming Ego.

Balance and common sense must be maintained in order to keep self-deception and egomania at bay. This is absolutely crucial to the magician's spiritual wellbeing.

LIBERATION FULFILLED

"When I speak here of Magic I have reference to the Divine Theurgy praised and reverenced by antiquity. It is of a quest spiritual and divine that I write; a task of self-creation and recreation, the bringing into human life of something eternal and enduring."
- Israel Regardie
from *The Tree of Life: An Illustrated Study in Magic*

So long as the magician avoids the perils mentioned earlier, the "Golden Journey" should be an infinitely rewarding one. Genuine magical initiation-where effects in the interior world have a significant impact on a person's life-is authentic and liberating. These are the initiations that change lives, sometimes in the most unexpected ways. The Path of Initiation, carefully and intelligently trodden, can be one of the most important steps taken by the spiritual rebel. In magic, the Initiate is expected to man the helm of his own ship. While others may check the compass and provide guidance, ultimately it is up to the individual magician to check the star-charts and set his or her course into the mystic.

TEAM PSYCHOPATH
Peter Conte

Gimme a "P"... gimme an "S"... gimme a ... wait... why am I going on like this? Revving you up, Kid. Gotta score. Gotta win. The big game–Your Life–hangs in the balance. You're the Team and this is Training Camp. If you're not looking, feeling, being sharp, you lose. And you're not a loser, are you?

The Opposition hates you. Holding you back, calling you strange, saying you're stupid, always kicking your meager ass, they can't stand that you're defiant, of them, and everything. The game has to be played their way and that's it. There's no room in their world for someone like you.

Tough, hey? You are different. They whack you one, you whack them back. They don't even know the meaning of pain. You're Hell on earth, and everyone and everything is the enemy.

Take it as it comes, give it back triple. Fight to the end.

Well, hopefully, the end is a long way off. You have a lot of terrorizing, er ... living, to do. And *The Black Books*[1] will help. This is the Game Plan and the Masters didn't write it just to watch you putz along. They expect you to execute, to attain, to evoke your Will, and wreak joyful havoc on the world around you. You can take all of the hints, rules, and slights on your character written in the *Black Books* and

---

[1] *The Black Books* (New Falcon Publications) comprise a multi-volume series of booklets written by Dr. Christopher S. Hyatt, Ph.D. that coincide with the teachings of the Extreme Individual Institute, which Hyatt founded. Following Dr. Hyatt's death in 2008 the EII was renamed as the New Extreme Individual Institute, and is a non-profit/prophet (ir)religious sleeper cell, dedicated to the furtherance of the work of the EII. (www.neweii.com)

actualize into a working marvel, a formidable Magician, a Psychopath. But you gotta be in shape.

What's your Team look like? Hell, Kid, like you. Mind, body, senses, emotions, that's your Team. And whether you like it or not, the Team has to be beaten into fighting shape. You gotta be cruel to be cruel. It's the Psychopath's way. The harder you are on yourself, the less the world can control you. The more personal pain applied to yourself, the stronger your Magick over the Food/Prey. Set your own pain threshold, the higher the better. Because you can take it, you will succeed. Time to fight, time to win, gotta get to it before time runs out. Go Team!

Coach sez: enough already Conte. Don't you ever get tired of sniffing your own Brain Farts?

Only a Star can lead the Team and that's your BMOC (Big Mind On Campus). You have the biggest Mind around. Just ask you. You'll tell them. The Psychopathic Mind is quick, incisive, and deadly, a seething volcano held on standby, capable of seeing everything and able to switch on automatically to act and counteract adjusting to the unfolding human drama progressing in real time while preparing a course of action to implement as to whatever will be happening in the next few seconds. And at the very best you won't even notice the Mind working. Properly trained, your Mind will calmly click on and guide the body around all obstacles, and then go back into Ready Mode. The Psychopath's Mind needs to be ever vigilant, to react quickly, and to handle many threats at the same time. Daydreaming is deadly. Do your daydreaming in your Alone Time where all scenarios of what can happen, what might go wrong, and what you really want can be computed. Dream big and imagine glory. Also, erase the past Imprinting that's ravaging your Mind. Mental baggage is a lead weight and slows your Team. Keep a blank

Mind in your present day circumstances to prevent further negative Imprinting. The only allowed Imprinting is your Mind programming for success.

Live in your daily life as usual with the stipulation of now you will be moving in a Psychopathic way. Take the training hints in the *Black Book* and win.

Observe only, don't think. Observing with a blank Mind allows for taking in and reacting to all the actions around you. Only actively think when confronted with a concrete problem, and then go back on standby again. It's more important to guide the senses then to dwell on the meaning of life. Your life is War.

The Brain is your CIC (Combat Information Center) that the Mind can trust to operate independently by virtue of the previous programming agreed to between them during operational exercises to set up the flow charts necessary to allow the Team to work as a whole. The less damage you do to your Brain, the better off you'll be. Alcohol, drugs, and bad Magick gone wrong dents the Brain, but, Hell, a Psychopath has to have a little fun, right?

The Brain seethes with electrical power. Try this exercise: when walking at night try to put the streetlights out. Later on, try to do this to a whole room. It will work and scare the hell out of people. You might get a minor headache, well; sometimes it's excruciating, but think of the power involved. Use this power in your Magical Workings.

Coach sez: keep your Game in the Mind.

The burning essence of everyone's Soul rests just inside the pupils of the Eyes. Power emanates outwards attacking all that comes in contact with their gaze and sucking in the wavering Wills of those caught in their trap. Normal eyesight talks of the person's Mind, Psychopathic eyesight is silent. Pull your vision awareness back in from the pupils.

This creates "quiet eyes" and no info will escape to tell what you're thinking.

Learn to have a "soft focus" (peripheral vision). This allows you see from ear to ear without anyone knowing that you're looking around. The more info you ingest, the better the Mind operates. Knowledge is power. Take in all you can see and give nothing away. In your Alone Time work on connecting the Eyes to the Brain so that the Mind can program them to perform the proper operations called for. Let your Eyes cast your Spells.

Coach sez: you can't spell Evil without the EYE.

The Nose is a psychic antenna able to sniff out the fears and desires of others. Try this exercise: turn off the other senses and let the Nose tell you what's going on around you.

Remember to breathe. If you're not breathing, you're probably dead and that can ruin all of the fun you expect to experience. Proper breathing exercises can help control the Mind and Body and mute your reactions to what others are doing to you.

Coach sez: know how to NOSE out the other Team's plays.

The Ears alert you as to what's happening around you from nearby to the far horizon. When they activate, they override all the other senses and send a message to the Mind to alert the Body to be ready in case defensive actions are called for. Constantly pounding the Ears with loud noises and music will severely damage them and leave you at a serious disadvantage.

Coach sez: tell those WIDE RECEIVERS to stay alert.

This triple threat combination of the Eyes, Nose, and Ears constitute your Early Warning System. By having a quiet essence about you, they can very effectively flare up individually or together and alert the Mind to all dangers.

Coach sez: D #.

The Mouth deals with Taste, Expressions, and Speech and is designated the Special Teams Package. The Star player is the Tongue. This tasteful little Devil is always in the thick of the action, and is a major pleasure center.

The naked, little Taste Buds chant "yum, yum, yum" as they come, come, come from whatever Mother Tongue has to offer when Father Mouth opens up and the sky is blotted out from all the delights that drop on to their seething world. They can go on forever. Beware the trap of the Space Masters who extol you to consume "Mass Quantities" as you could become Jabba the Hutt.

Coach sez: have a TASTE for the Good Life.

As a Signal Center to the world, the Lips let others know whether to approach or stay away, and the Emotional or Psychological state that you're going through at the moment.

Liken the Lips to the hiking of the ball, when they move the face follows. Only extreme effort can keep the Lips from reacting to what the Eyes see. When the Mind has concrete control of all operations, then are the Lips silent, but you'll be accused of having a dour attitude and a droll sense of humor.

Coach sez: tell'em to wrap their LIPS around this!

It is said Speech separates Humans from the rest of the creatures on this Planet. Not so. Have you never had a cat screech at you for its dinner? But Selective Speech does separate the Psychopath from the rest of the world. Whereas the Food/Prey babbles on, the Psychopath knows the secret of the Five Second Rule. Whatever you think, feel, or want to say, wait five seconds before you actually speak. That way you're not one of the babbling idiots whose words are unnecessary, inane, or end up ignored, and you'll either look like a genius from the validity of your point or your words were going to be babble so you kept quiet.

In fact, the less you say the more power you'll retain. Use your words to guide the conversation and by such the Food/Prey in the direction you want things to go. Use speech as a battering ram, drop subtle comments, invoke humor to entrance, tease, cajole, vary your cadence, and so on. Work out patterns in your Alone Time. Some styles of communication will be easy for you. Stick with them. Overcome fear with a Public Speaking class, or get a sales counter job where you have to deal with the public.

Large gatherings are the Psychopath's hunting ground. Well, they're everyone's hunting ground, but it depends on how you view them. The air is filled with crescendos of loud yapping. Usually, when the Mouth is moving, the Mind is closed down. Control your Speech. The Psychopath must keep the Ears open for guide words like the NSA does. A key word will alert you as to the presence of a Food/Prey. Hear, and then hunt.

Being out in the world might have you banging your head off the wall, but too much Alone Time is worse. All living creatures need to talk. Our words are the footpaths that lead us along from one moment to the next. Let your words be incisive.

Coach sez: We'll Kill'em with the RUN and SHOOT.

There's nothing you can do about the Weather, or your

Moods. Rarely good, almost always depressing, a Mood can settle on you from out of nowhere. When it hits, you're out of commission, hopefully for not that long. Even a Psychopath is human (unfortunately).

Coach sez: Goddamn Rain.

Your fan Base, the Emotions, love you, sometimes. Living vicariously through you, they expect a win, but usually they're not helping things. All your hard work for control can be ripped apart in an instant by their selfish hungers. This screaming crowd seethes about demanding your immediate attention. Rage, love, happiness, despair, lust, gluttony, and an infinite viper's den wearing your colors roots for you, but they're only on your side if you give them precedence over the others.

They scream out their existence to the world, me, me, me! The sudden violent force they exert takes over the Game. One of these monsters is enough; let alone having a multitude manifest at the same time. When they rear their screeching heads, you're no longer the Hunter, but something to be avoided.

A Hermetic exercise to help control these Demons is to imagine you have a Pendulum in your Mind that will swing to and fro when you get emotional. If you don't let yourself get too far UP when you're excited, then you won't get that far DOWN when things go wrong. Control your swing when good things are happening even though this mutes the level of happiness. You can't control the DOWN side of the swing on its own. The Pendulum can be made to have a tight swing. You'll only be as DOWN as you let yourself get UP.

By establishing control over the Emotions, then you can conjure them up whenever you want. It can be mighty exciting, for you, not the Food/Prey, when you go through your roladex and pick out an Emotion to display. It'll scare the Hell out of them, leaving them wondering "where did that come from?" This might be considered "playing with your food." Sudden Emotional outbursts, controlled with the connivance of the Mind, will create confusion in the Food/Preys and this is one of the Psychopath's feeding zones. It's fun to go crazy at the push of a button.

Coach sez: look at those Crazy Bastards. At least they're good for the Beer Sales.

Your "LOOK" is your Uniform, which sets the Style of how you appear to the world. From the wildest eccentricity to the conformity to your selected group, the Psychopath is adamant that "things" must be "just right" Color (black?, again?) of clothing, type of jewelry, hair style, accessories (do something about those shoes, Kid), all scream in the face of the world at large, the world the Psychopath rebels from, but is all this excess really rebellion?

It could be that a white T-shirt and blue jeans might just make you the most dangerous person around. The true Psychopathic Hunter embraces invisibility, and if you look "lame" that's all they'll notice about you, and then no one will fear you, and that's when everyone should be very, very afraid. They won't know where their whackings are coming from.

But that probably won't be the case. The Psychopath, especially an Occult one, has to have at least a little "weirdness." Just remember, the badges and codes shown on your LOOK alert the Roll Models as to who and what you are, and make it easy for "the Man" to bust your balls. If you exert all your energy fighting, you'll not be able to feed in peace.

Wearing Gothic in a Goth crowd is conformity. Wearing Gothic in a Brooks Brother's crowd stands out. Wearing Brooks Brother's in a Goth crowd is Psychopathic. Or you can a get a Tattoo.

Coach sez: do that Crazy End Zone Dance.

Your Quirks are your Playbook, Kid. What'a ya got? Do you stand like a lump, or flash green at the Bartender? If the line isn't moving, is it you holding things up? Work the Red Zone. How you use your Body sets you apart from all the other Psychopaths. Run some good Routes.

Coach sez: dazzle 'em with the ol' Shake and Bake.

The Game will be played on the Field of Action, your Body. There's not a lot you can do about how your Body looks. Deal with what you got. A huge Body can be graceful, and a lithe one klutzy. You don't have to be comfortable about your shape, just confident from that Psychopathic inner vibe. Motion, with attitude, allows you to shine.

Your Body is you-in-the-world. Your Flesh seeks other Flesh to actualize its existence. It's the way of Nature. Often, ignoring better judgment, it seeks some down and dirty action. You'll have to be a great Grounds keeper to get it back in to somewhat pristine shape, but don't worry about wearing it out.

From the moment of your Birth, your cells have raged a War between Life and Death. Whether you lock yourself in a room, or ingest all of the poisons available to you, there is nothing you can do to halt your inevitable demise. Buck up, Kid, all of us are Walking Corpses. So, allow your Body to enjoy total fulfillment, for it'll be staying here even as the Mind travels on to a Better Game.

Coach sez: the Game was decided by SUDDEN DEATH.

Listen up, Kid, this is the Unhappy Recap. No one's rooting for you. What you gain, they lose. You're on your own. Gotta grab with some gusto everything you want. Their only hope is that you'll wake up tomorrow and play the same lame game. Gimme a "P"... gimme an "S"...

Coach sez: hehehe...

Hypatia of Alexandria

Lon Milo DuQuette

DEVIL BE MY GOD

Lon Milo DuQuette

Author (or coauthor) of the New Falcon Publication titles:
The Enochian World of Aleister Crowley: Enochian Sex Magic
Sex Magick, Tantra and Tarot: The Way of the Secret Lover
Aleister Crowley's Illustrated Goetia: Sexual Evocation

"I advise you to curb that waging tongue of yours."
–Bishop of the Black Connons

"It's a habit I've never formed Your Grace."
–Robin Hood

In A.D. 415 Cyril, the Bishop of Alexandria Egypt, found himself in a most awkward position. Not only was he burdened with the task of concocting viable doctrines[1] from the muddled and conflicting traditions of the young Christian cult, he was required to do so in the most sophisticated and enlightened pagan city on earth.

Long before the alleged virgin birth of the crucified savior, Alexandria, with her celebrated schools and library, nurtured the greatest minds of the Mediterranean world and Asia. Here, religion and philosophy were lovers, and their union gave rise to dynamic environment of dialog and debate. On more than one occasion Cyril tried to glean converts from the student body of the Neo-Platonic Academy, only to be stuck dumb by the discomforting realization that the fledgling philosophers

---

[1] Cyril is credited with formulating the concept of the Holy Trinity, an invention for which he was eventually canonized.

were far more knowledgeable than he about the subtleties and shortcomings of his own faith. Uncomfortable as he such moments were His Grace bore them dutifully. They afforded him the opportunity to suffer for his faith. His patience came to an end, however, when his faith and reputation were challenged by a brilliant and charismatic luminary of the Alexandrian School of Neo-Platonism, Hypatia–the greatest woman initiate of the ancient world.

Hypatia of Alexandria was without question the most respected and influential thinker of her day. The daughter of the great mathematician, Theon, she took over her father's honored position at the Academy and lectured there for many years. She, more than any other individual since Plotinus, the father of Neo-Platonism, grasped the profound potential of that school of thought. Her lectures were wildly popular and attracted a stream of scholars who was in Ne-Platonism the possibility of a truly universal spiritual order–a supreme philosophy–an enlightened religion to unite all religions. Such was the golden promise of Neo-Platonism, and Hypatia of Alexandria was its virgin prophetess.

Troubled by the continued degeneration of the Christian movement, its intolerance of other faiths and its dangerous preoccupation with miracles and wonders, Hypatia began a series of public lectures dealing with the cult. She revealed the pagan roots of the faith and systematically unmasked the absurdities and superstitions that had infected the movement. Then, with power and eloquence surpassing that of any Christian apologist, she elucidated upon what she understood to be the true spiritual treasures found in the purported teachings of the "Christ."

Her arguments were so persuasive that many new converts to the cult renounced their conversions and became disciples of Hapatia. Her lectures stimulated enormous interest in Christianity, but not Christianity as it was presented by Cyril, the Bishop of Alexandria.

Not blessed with the strength of character necessary to suffer a personal confrontation with Hypatia, Cryil embarked upon a campaign of personal vilification by preaching to his unwashed and fanatical flock that Hypatia was a menace to the faith, a sorceress in league with the Devil. These diatribes seemed to have little effect upon the sophisticated population of urban Alexandria who were beginning to realize that Bishop Cyril's Christianity was a cult that didn't play well with other children. Deep in the Nitrian dessert, however, Cyril's hateful words eventually reached the crude monastery of Peter the Reader.

Years of preaching to the wind and converting scorpions had uniquely qualified Peter to be the cleansing sword of the Prince of Peace, and the though of a devil-possessed woman attacking his savior was more than this man of God could stomach. Mustering a rag-tag collection of fellow hermits, he marched to Alexandria where they met with officials of the Caesarean church who informed him that each afternoon the shameless Hypatia drove her own chariot from the Academy to her home. Armed only with clubs, oyster shells, and the Grace of God, Peter and his mob ambushed Hypatia in the street near the Academy. Pulling her from her chariot they dragged her to her Caesarean church where they stripped her, beat her with clubs, and finally (because of an on-going debate over the soul's eternal status if the corpse remained whole) scraped the flesh from her bones with the oyster shells. The scoops of flesh and the rest of her remains were then carried away and burned.

The reaction of the Alexandrian community was one of confusion and shock, and the Neo-Platonist school was dealt a blow from which it never recovered. Although he went to great lengths to distance himself from the incident, Cyril took full advantage of the situation and used the terror of the moment to further intimidate the city and establish that the will of the Christian God was to be resisted at one's own risk.

The martyrdom of Hypatia was certainly not the first example of truth resisting evil and losing, but it did mark the beginning of a prolonged spiritual delirium tremor from which Western Civilization has never fully recovered. Even the bright souls who did not succumb to the universal madness were forced to blossom against the twisted projections of the collective nightmare.

Spiritual growth is not impossible in such an environment. But where wisdom is perceived by the world to be ignorance; love is considered sin, and all that is best in the human spirit is condemned and repressed, the road by which a seeker of enlightenment must travel takes many curious turns. On such a journey one's companions are outlaws and rebels; sacredness breeds in blaspheme, truth falls from the lips of false prophets, heaven is sought in hell, and God is the Devil himself.

BREAKING TRANCE

Steven Heller, Ph.D.

Author of the New Falcon Publication title:
*Monsters and Magical Sticks:
There's No Such Thing As Hypnosis?*

How do you know when you're getting too close to a fire? Of course, by feeling the heat! But what if you were unable to feel the heat? You would probably not know until you were burning yourself or you smelled your flesh burning. So many people go through life in such a deep trance, that they do not know when they are heading for trouble until they have stepped into it. They no longer know what they feel, want or need!

A small child hears his/her parents fighting and becomes afraid. They tell conflicting stories and she/he becomes confused. They send out incongruent messages and the anxiety rises to painful levels. One day she/he discovers that by "dropping out" and going off into inner-space-out, everything is better... for a while. If I can't feel it, hear it or see it, it can't get me. TRANCE IS BORN! Of course, if a truck is coming at you and you respond by "Not seeing or hearing it" I guarantee that you will feel it. Your trance will simply prevent you from getting out of the way.

A child enters a new and exciting world called school. S/he is curious and open to learning. "Children, we must all sit just like this and always raise your hand and there is one right way to do things and of course only one right answer!" says the adult called teacher. Day in and day out s/he sees things but is told they don't really exist. S/he feels things and is told that the feelings are not real and s/he doesn't really know what s/he feels in the first place. The secret of survival? Go into a trance! The result...years later s/he doesn't feel what there is to feel, can't hear what there is to hear and can't see what needs to be seen. Frustration, failure and pain is a constant companion.

The secret...*BREAK TRANCE!* You must learn to question and question some more. You cannot trust what you have been tranced into seeing, hearing, or feeling. Tonight, when you go to sleep, sleep on the other side of the be; sit at a different seat at meal times. For the adventurous, eat with your left hand (or right hand if you are left-handed). Read a book...from the last page; record conversations with those you have the poorest communication with. Look for problem area instead of avoiding them and then come up with three of the most unusual methods for solving the problem. Put a rubber band on your wrist and snap it when ever you feel yourself "dropping out."

Learn to talk to those parts of you that know the difference between trance and what is happening around you. For example, imagine that you begin to feel anxiety. Ask your inner guide to change the feeling into a picture; first a picture of what the feeling itself looks like, and then ask that part to change the picture into one that will help you discover what is really happening for (or to) you. Learn to hear the sound of colors and feelings and to see the feelings and sounds. In short, shake up your systems and break your patterns. (For many interesting and provocative methods of breaking trance, you might even purchase my book, *Monsters and Magical Sticks: There's No Such Thing As Hypnosis*.) Last, but not least, find a good hypnotist who will help you to use hypnosis and trance in order to end your hypnotic trance.

THE BLACK ART OF PSYCHOTHERAPY
Dr. Jack S. Willis

The multi entendre of the title is intentional and appropriate (multi: more than double, less than many). Let us count the ways.

First, psychotherapy is an art. It is not a science (the human-beings-are-laboratory-rats mentality of the behaviorists notwithstanding). A friend of mine, a philosopher of esthetics, defines art as: anything that people treat as art. So it is with psychotherapy. Any mad school that springs up and that gets people to call it "psychotherapy" then becomes a "psychotherapy." But is it good psychotherapy or just mad? We will return to that.

Second of the entendre is that, by whatever definition, it is a black art. And, in two ways. First, it supposedly deals with the dark side of the person. Call it dark, call it hidden, call it black; by whatever name, it is the devil within us that is awakened in psychotherapy. Second, as an art, it is dependent not only on the artistry of the practitioner, but also on the (en)light(enment) of the therapist. We will return to that, too.

Third of the entendre, it is a black art because, examined closely, it employs the same techniques, albeit in different robes, as does thaumaturgy and invocation of the spirits. The names of the spirits are different, and the drugs are (usually) different, and the invocation rituals are different; but it is magic nonetheless. And black magic at that.

Do you wish to move to a different plane of consciousness? Try hypnosis or alpha wave biofeedback or sodium amytal or any number of emotion altering drugs. Do you wish to feel fully? Try Gestalt or psycho-drama or Primal. Do you wish to probe the unknown and unknowable. Try Jungian. Do you wish a re-birth? Try Rankian, or rebirthing, or age regression (even to rebirth in former lives). Do you wish to be loved? Try Rogerian. Is death your issue? Existentialist therapy awaits. Or, perhaps you want better sex or mind-body unity? Try Reichian, Bio-energetics, Feldenkrais, Rolf or Alexander technique. For every passion there is a therapy, and for every therapy there is a passionate following. What to do? What to do? We will return to that, too. There is an answer.

Final of the entendre, it is also an art of the patient (really a student rather than a patient). The art of the student is where we will finish our exploration.

Psychotherapy As Art

No two people are alike. A photograph as art can be duplicated an infinite number of times. Similarly an etching. A bronze can be recast. But people are ever unique and ever changing. The interchange between therapist and student is a ballet. Is there a leader and a follower? The can be; there doesn't have to be. But one thing of this dance is certain: if the therapist can only dance to his own tune, if he is committed to a school and a technique irrespective of the student, then the ballet will be an awkward and even disastrous performance.

How then does the student choose a teacher? How can you judge your teachers artistic sensibility? I will answer the choice of teacher question here and wait until later to address the question of his artistry. The answer to choosing a teacher is easy, if not obvious. There are two questions to ask: (1) what is your objective and (2) what is your time line. Put it this way: if you exercise, do you want a little workout once or twice a week or do you want to really tone your muscles? Do you want to exercise until you lose 10 pounds, or do you want to make it a part of your life? What is your objective and what is your time line? If your objective is limited and/or you want quick answers, then choose a teacher whose method is quick and direct. Rational emotive therapy, hypnosis, cognitive-behavioral or behaviorism are good answers.

If your objective is to increase your happiness quotient, to correct your errors in living, to exercise the daemons inside you, then choose a teacher who increases anxiety. If your teacher promises to love you unconditionally, run. If your teacher tells you that he is problem oriented, run. If your teacher tells you that he will deal with your emotions but not with your thinking, run. If he says he deals with the here-and-now not with the past, sprint. If he says he is only a (fill in the school) therapist and that is the only school he believes in, find a new teacher. There is no sense in finding a teacher of French when you are planning a trip to Germany.

But, since nothing in life is easy, if he says he is totally flexible, that he is eclectic, that he uses whatever is appropriate with no commitment to any theory, then make a mad dash. In psychotherapy, the word eclectic is often a synonym "for I don't know what I am doing, I just do whatever feels right."

If your objective is long-term personal growth, then choose the teacher whose statement to you make you anxious, unsettled, nervous, unsure. Therein lies an answer.

The Dark Side of Our Soul

I will make the, I think very reasonable, assumption that anyone who reads this book is interested in maximizing their potential and increasing their productivity and creativity. For such a person therapy is a Godsend (to steal a metaphor). My teacher, Israel Regardie (and Dr. Hyatt) said that he would not teach anyone the methods of the Golden Dawn unless they had had at least 4 years of Reichian therapy. Regardie took that position for a very good reason. Until we have removed some of the darkness within our own soul, any attempt at thaumaturgy will only evoke our own indwelling devils. Freud said that repression and sublimation were necessary for one to live in the society. Reich claimed the only answer was to change society. I am less pessimistic then those two towering figures.

When they were writing, we did not have the knowledge of the developmental steps of the ego and we did not have the work of Piaget on children's cognitive development. I've proven it enough times to enough students; that I can say with some confidence that the main issue in our personal psychology is mistakes in thinking. As children we attempted to understand the silly (sometimes crazy, sometimes evil) statement and actions of our parents. However, children and adults live in different worlds of knowledge and thinking. What seems obvious to a parent, is adult babble to a child. Parents pretend that they are teaching the child to...(behave, to considerate, share, be polite, etc.) when in truth all they are doing is confusing the child. The child tries to make sense out of the teaching, misunderstands most of what is taught; and neither the child nor the parent knows how off the two are.[1]

Human beings are magnificent but flawed creatures. We take the mistakes of childhood, we live them our whole life, we never recognize they were wrong to begin with, and that they are now doubly wrong as adults. Thus we live our lives in war with ourselves. It is a terrible waste of energy. We take

---

[1] My favorite story is the mother who yells at her child to not play with the lamp because he will break it. A moment later, and CRASH! So, "I told you not to play with the lamp, now look what you've done!" But, says the bright child, "I wasn't playing with the lamp, I was playing with the spaceship." Children live in different cognitive universes than do adults.

the glory and the beauty of the infant and create anger and misery of the adult. It is to take a David of Michelangelo and re-sculpt him into a Henry Moore burdened and struggling tortured soul.

It doesn't need to be, it shouldn't be. Freud said, where the id was, there the ego shall be. I would say where darkness was there light shall be.

The (En)Light(enment) Of The Therapist

There is a danger in psychotherapy. The danger is called the therapist. The therapist is the magician of this black art. When he attempts to exorcise your devils is he doing it by inserting his own? In psychological terms, is he attempting to project his own devils into you? And how can you tell if he is?

There is no infallible answer to this one. There are some guides. How much therapy has your proposed therapist had (minimum of 7 years)? What kind of therapy(ies) did he have? Is he attempting to use a particular school of therapy in which he has not himself been a patient If so, choose another teacher. You can ignore licenses and degrees. They mean nothing. What matters is the knowledge of and therapy experience of your proposed therapist, not what degrees or licenses he does or does not have. In how many schools of therapy is he knowledgeable? The minimum is two. But here is the most important rule of all: if the therapist talks about himself (other than to answer your questions) or he frequently brings in how he feels or would feel in your situation then he is definitely trying to work out his own problems on your time. You have come upon a dark soul (irrespective of or in spite of any therapy he may have had). Stop now. You are with the wrong teacher. Darkness cannot create lightness of being.

Choosing A Therapist

It may seem like I have talked of little else. But the subject is not exhausted. As a Reichian therapist of nearly 30 years experience, there is more that can be added. As you may know, Reichian therapy is a body approach to therapy. Therefore, we get a lot of information from the physical appearance, the gestures, the voice tone, the eyes, etc. Here, then, are some tips from the Reichian couch. Your therapist should have forehead creases. The should not be permanent (a furrowed brow), they should become prominent when the eyebrows are raised and, except or the crease, disappear when the eyebrows are lowered. His eyes should be clear, very focused, and they should move easily. There should be a definite nasal-labial line (the line from the corner of the nose to the corner of the mouth). The neck muscles should not be prominent. The voice should be resonant, coming firm an open throat rather than a constricted one. If he takes a big breath, both the belly and the chest should move. Of the things I have listed here, the most important is the forehead and the eyes. If his eyes are dull or they do not move easily or his forehead has no crease lines or has permanent creases, quit now. What if you have been making wonderful progress with just this kind of therapist? My suggestion: take a six-month vacation from this therapist and look into some others. The vacation will be good for you anyway and the experience of some visits to other teachers might give you some perspective on his virtues and his failings.

If you have not chosen a therapist, or if you are going to take a vacation, here is my suggestion: There are four good schools of depth therapy: psychodynamic, ego psychology (also called object relations), neo-Freudian, and Reichian. Note that the word is *psychodynamic*, not *psychoanalysis*. The foundation is the same, but the technique is very different.

Notwithstanding that Jungian is very popular among the readers of New Falcon Publications, I would urge against it. I have yet to see good results emerge from Jungian analysis. Stay as far away as possible from Primal therapy or any variant. Adlerian, in the right hands, is an acceptable alternative; but then go to someone else afterwards to get to the areas that Adlerian can not address. Bio-energetics is not bad except that you walk around angry for years, in the process losing marriages, jobs, and friends. Existential therapy can be done well, but it is rare. Most therapists proclaiming themselves as existentialist have not done the study necessary to make good use of the art. Existentialist is not one school; it is a whole bunch with differing degrees of worth. Of all the rest, I would say: Ignore them. They are not depth therapy, and they can not do the job you deserve.

The Art Of The Patient

Now, finally, to the most important part: **YOU!** Even a truly good teacher is no good if the student will not study, if the student will not do his homework. If you are not important to your self why should you be important to your therapist? Is it rational to expect that your therapist will work hard for you when you will not work hard for yourself?

Here is a statement that you have probably never heard any therapist make: the two most important qualities that you need to bring to the study are *anger* and *courage*. Anger in the form of the demand of yourself, the commitment, that you will not settle for less than you can be. You will not settle for injuring your children because you have not uncovered your own daemons. You will not settle for less productivity, less creativity, less enjoyment of the wonder of life than is possible for you to achieve. That does not mean that your goal is perfection. We leave that realm to the Gods. It does mean that however much you can uncover, understand, and correct is the minimum you will settle for and the devil take the hindmost. Then there is courage. Daemons are scary creatures. What are your daemons? Are they depression, anxiety, anger, guilt, facing the fact that your parents are not the nice people you want them to be, realizing that you have been living your life for other people and not for yourself, realizing that you are not as important as you want to think you are, realizing that you made a bad choice in a mate, realizing that you have been pretending to enjoy sex? For all your determination to surrender the darkness for the light, you have to have the courage to stay the course, confess the big and the little, accept that you are what you are–not what you want to be, and most of all: the determination to accept that the losses of your childhood are permanent losses. That last one is a biggie and it raises another factor.

Intellectual integrity should be another part of your art. A man of intellectual integrity does not attempt to fake reality. *What is, simply is.* It is not subject to our fantasies, our wishes, or our ideals. It is not pretty or ugly. It is not noble or ignoble. It is not heroic or cowardly. It simply is. As honesty is telling the truth to others, so integrity is telling the truth to ourselves. It is much harder. We know when we are lying to someone else. *But the lies we tell our self are the lies we live by.* They are part of our very being. And they are corrosive.

There is much that could be said here, but there is only one thing I want to add. Never accept anything your therapist says except as a possibility to *honestly examine.* Your own mind is the ultimate judge of the validity of any idea or interpretation. Yes, you are student to this teacher because you can not uncover your own errors of thinking. But the alternative is not to turn your mind over to someone else.

Your therapist may or may not be an advanced soul, an enlightened person. He may have penetrating insights, and he may be "a wise man" (as the Talmudists would say). And, certainly, you are in his office to take a graduate degree in living. Certainly his explanations and interpretations deserve a respectful audience. But, in the end, it is our trained judgment that is the authority. Your therapist can demand all he wants that he is right because he is the therapist/authority. Do not buy it. On the subject of you, you are the authority. Take every idea he puts forth, examine it with anger, courage, and integrity, and then, if it is wrong, discard it. Your life is a temple. It deserves respect, reverence, and prayer; don't let it go to waste, it is too sacred.

ANOTHER BEDTIME STORY
Dr. William S. Hyatt, Ph.D.

Our story starts in the living room of Sam Simple, a carpet salesman who is twenty-nine-years-old. Sam lives with his wife Tammy in the last stronghold of racism and muddle-dum-Burbank, California.

When Sam and Tammy first met-three years ago at a dance club in Hollywood–they fell in "love at first sight." The romantic couple quickly moved in together and soon after, married. While the romance was brewing, Sam continually assured himself and his friends that his relationships with them would not change. He would not stop being independent, he would not forget his old pals, he would not spend all of his time with his new wife. Of course, Sam did forget his friends, he did forget his autonomy, and he did forget his promises.

Although Sam told me that he really loved Tammy, and that she was "perfect," I wondered what sort of powerful drug he had taken which made him lose sight of reality and forget all of the promises that he had made.

As Sam and Tammy's relationship grew, so did Sam's Visa bill. They bought new furniture–antiques, because they hold their value, was the rationalization that I was given. New clothes, actually "vintage clothes;' a new term coined by people who sell old clothes. And they both started hobbies, collecting various types of bric-a-brac. These items were bought because Sam and Tammy wanted to show their friends that they were different, and of course superior. They bought new cars, or old cars that had been fixed up to look "perfect." They did make one strange concession to the future, they moved into a new–yes, a brand new-apartment complex; one which had no previous smells in the carpet.

In the new apartment the young couple had found a home. They started decorating. First they put up lace curtains (from Wards). Then they bought towels to match their toilet seat cover. Soon they bought antique furniture. An old free-standing radio that didn't work very well, but was very pretty. Sam bought old phones, from the 1930s. These phones also didn't work very well. They were hard to dial, hard to use and bulky, but again, they conveyed the uniqueness of Sam and Tammy's existence.

As the young couple started to put their scent everywhere in the house, they felt more and more at home. Tammy started collecting 1930s sheet music, which she framed and hung above the old radio, and soon Sam bought an old Victrola, which when played sounded like a dozen cats getting mauled by a starving pit bull.

As the couple added more and more "things" to their home, they became more and more unhappy. Were these possessions a mere substitute for the empty feelings in their lives? Sam started changing jobs, as did Tammy. They both started eating health food and taking more than fifty vitamins each, every day. Tammy sold her car and bought a new Ford, while Sam had his vintage VW bug repainted. Sam sold his 1930s fully restored wristwatch in favor of a new Timex. When the Timex broke, he bought a 1960s Omega, gold-tone.

Sam and Tammy were through nest building, they had filled their nest with many toys and were looking at Visa payments, rent and auto expenses that took ninety percent of their combined net incomes. Should they start a family or start a hobby?

Although Sam "forgot" about his previous promises to himself and his friends, he did take a firm stand on one conviction: "I hate kids and will not have them:' Although Tammy verbally went along with this mandate, she even said that she was incapable of having kids, she secretly wanted to fill her nest. Would the remaining ten percent of the couple's income support the next generation of nest-builders and antique collectors?

When Sam arrived home from work one day, he was surprised to find a note from "mom," aka Tammy. It said, "I am at doctor Rothenberg's office, will be back by five." As Sam sat around and wondered what sort of ailment befell his simple wife, he started to grind his teeth. When Tammy walked in the front door, she exclaimed that she was pregnant, as if no one on earth had ever been pregnant before. But, she was more than pregnant–somehow she had been transformed. She had a look in her eyes, a look that said: "I am a mother in training, now I am an expert."

Sam went crazy. His teeth stopped grinding. He broke pictures, vases, records and even broke a blood vessel. He knew that he must take a stand. He had lied to himself about everything since he had been married, and he knew that he couldn't tolerate this major breech of conduct on the part of his wife. He told Tammy that if she wanted to have the baby fine, but that he would leave within the hour. Otherwise, she should turn right back around, and ask Dr. Rothenberg to perform an abortion, immediately.

When Tammy left the house crying, Sam was alone in his living room.

He stood staring at his mannequins dressed in World War I German military uniforms. These mannequins had become his children. They didn't eat or talk back. They didn't require time, unless one wanted to give it, and best of all they were UNIQUE-like Sam.

The one on the right side of the room was dressed in a blue enlisted man's dress uniform, with a red sash across his chest. The brass buttons were shined every week, as were the many medals. The white pants were starched and pressed and the long sword hung powerfully to the right side. The highlight of the outfit was the spiked helmet, which was on the mannequin's head. The helmet was a shiny black shell with an impressive brass plate of an eagle clutching a saber adorning its front. The tall and glossy spike rose smartly above the helmet. This spike might be the esoteric German phallic symbol, in the form of a six inch pointed spike, rising out of someone's hand. The left side of the room contained a life-size statue of the Jack-in-the-Box. He was also dressed in a German spiked helmet, although he was lacking the matching uniform. Covering the walls were pictures of German soldiers in ancient battles. Prussians firing old cannons at helpless natives, and a framed picture of Himmler, with the following caption: "A great man, one who served his country and followed orders, no matter how much he personally opposed them." Was Himmler an earlier version of Oliver North?

As Sam sat and thought of his life, he wondered if a child meant he would have to give up his precious collection of German/Prussian artifacts. He decided that it did, a thought he couldn't stand. "The baby would have to sleep in this room. It would cry all night long. And most importantly, I would have to sell all of my toys to keep it in diapers."

He hoped that Tammy would make the right decision. When she came home in tears, all Sam could think of was his collection of military relics: "Did you do it?" He gasped. When she started crying again, he knew that she had, and he was relieved. Now he could keep buying his junk/toys and more importantly-he could tell his friends that he stood up for his rights: "I told her what to do, and she ain't going to have no kid in my house.'"

The next week Sam made a visit to his doctor. That night he told his wife that he had made a statement of his individuality, "I got myself fixed:' Now when Tammy talks to Sam about planning for the future, children are never discussed, instead they talk about new uniforms, sheet music, old cars and a bigger nest. And, Sam has again shown how unique he really is.

The scene now moves to Pasadena California. We move into the lives of Melvin and Dodie Weiss, another couple recently married. They too are unique, but in a different way.

Melvin is an elitist, like Sam, although he is an intellectual one. His young wife Dodie, nineteen-years-old, thinks that everyone is equal...she isn't very bright. Dodie looks a bit like a bowling ball. She is four-foot-ten in height, while weighing about one hundred forty-eight pounds. She has typical Jewish features, highlighted by ugly frizzy hair, which is closely cropped and covered with a light dandruffy frost. The many birth marks which adorn her face look like a map of war-torn Europe. Like Tammy, Dodie wears old clothes, but she buys them at the Goodwill, as it is the only place she can afford to shop. Also like the Simples, the Weisses have a lot of old junk, but not by choice; they simply can't afford new junk yet.

Melvin doesn't love or respect his wife, but she is eighteen years younger than him, and very fertile. Melvin hypothesizes that his wife thinks all people are equal because she is a moron, and because she looks like a bowling ball. He doesn't mind Dodie's looks, as he is no better looking himself. In fact, he looks a bit like a bowling pin. Melvin is tall, with wide hips and no visible hair on his arms or legs. His face seems to lack features, unless you strain to find his dull eyelids. Melvin and Dodie, they seem to be a happy and well matched couple.

Dodie, a natural Jew, has many important opinions to share. Although Melvin tells her that opinions are like assholes, everyone has them, ultimately he agrees with everything that her small mind can conjure up; he does this since he can't seem to convince her to accept any of his views. Either they are too complex or she is too narrow in her world view. The first opinion she tells her new husband, is they must plan for their future. They should buy grave plots at Mount Sinai, so that they can be together forever, or at least until some developer builds condos on the property. Next, Dodie convinces Melvin that he should work two jobs so that they can make payments on their land, and send her to school at the same time. Meanwhile, they live in a seedy, roach-filled apartment in the ghetto of Pasadena. Melvin drives an ancient VW bug that always starts, but that has no heat, windows or padding in the seats. While Dodie takes the bus all over the Los Angeles area.

While Dodie and Melvin are struggling as students and planning for their future, they continually reassure each other that they are unique. They certainly are a perfect match, after all bowling pins and bowling balls often go together.

Dodie tells anyone who will listen that she doesn't value material things (is this because she doesn't have any?) but only her husband and future family. She tells anyone who will listen that when she graduates she will go to work as a teacher, forgetting the fact that she has been fired from twelve jobs in the last eighteen months. Dodie's plans continue: when the family has a double income, they will move to the mountains and buy a piece of land, (no, not another grave plot) so that they can build their dream box; no, I mean house. This dream house will enable the youngsters to raise a family and be secure, safe and trapped.

Although Melvin feels that his grave plot and his dream house are somehow closely related, he can't figure out how. He is very busy working three jobs now, so he isn't able to understand that he has become a tool for his wife's whims.

Dodie wants to surround herself with clutter and junk, although not the kind that Sam and Tammy have, the kind that cries in the night. Soon, she will be able to justify everything that she does, including the following of her whims, for the sake of her children. She will surround herself with activities, such as knitting groups, women's groups and co-op babysitting groups. She will pretend that all of her friends are equal to her, while she secretly judges them, thereby making herself feel superior. Most uniquely, Dodie will become an instant expert on child rearing. She will tell her weak-willed husband that they will raise their children differently, better, wiser and with better results. She will tell him of all of her plans for accomplishing these goals, and how brilliant they are.

Although Melvin will try to leave Dodie before they get to the reproduction scene, he will soon come back to her, as he won't be able to make it on his own; without his "mommy" to make his plans. In turn, Dodie will have a nervous breakdown, as she worries that she has not been fertilized yet. She secretly wonders if she can find any other man dumb enough to nest with her. After all, her plans are very unique.

The earth is a giant egg. It is waiting to be fertilized again. Who will do it? Sam, a man for all seasons, who lives in the past, as a way of avoiding the future. Or will Melvin, a man who understands the secrets of the universe. Melvin knows that everything is related to either the crack in someone's ass or the crack in the cosmic egg, but he can't figure out which one is more correct.

Should we get a diaper for the planet or for the people on the planet? Should we get a diaper for the unborn eggs or should we re-fertilize again? Should we collect war relics or start new wars? Should we believe that we are unique or should we attempt to understand language limitations? Should we build new nests in the mountains or should we build future nests in the cemetery? Should we go to college or should we sell carpet? Should we buy new cars or drive old ones? Should we paint our old cars and call them classic or should we leave them alone and call them junk? Should we marry bowling balls or marry bowling pins? Finally, should we delude ourselves with whims, fantasy and societal customs or should we find a new egg to inhabit and new lives to fertilize?

What we can learn from the true tale of Sam/Tammy and Melvin/Dodie, is that people attempt to place themselves in an illusory place of uniqueness and self-importance. Further, this is done primarily through the misuse of language. Language is the prisoner, the jailer, the warden and the cell. Language is also the crime. With language we delude ourselves, delude others and build a false wall of illusion around our lives and actions. Because Sam calls his VW or his clothes vintage, they are better than Melvin's who has a junk VW (same year-1963) and old clothes. Who is superior? Who is more unique? The very notion of distinguishing the difference between the two and judging which is superior is ludicrous. In fact, the notion of superiority and uniqueness is just another example of limiting language.

THE GREEK RITUAL OF MAGIC

Dr. Israel Regardie
Appendix II from **Ceremonial Magic**
A Guide To The Mechanisms of Ritual
New Falcon Publications, First Edition 2022

This essay was written over eighty-five years ago. It was published first in *The Occult Review* in London, and recently was republished by Gareth Knight in his excellent periodical *New Dimensions*.

It is included in this book, not because of the simple fact that it is about dramatic rituals, but because in a larger sense *all* rituals are dramatic, at least they should be in order to be effective. This is evidenced, for example, in the Eucharistic ritual on an earlier page, based on fundamental simple formulae that eventuate in a dramatic climax.

The word 'dramatic' as here used implies only that type of ritual or ceremony in which several celebrants are used, as it were, as in the theatre. The ritual elaborated on this essay, based on Gilbert Murray's superb translation of *The Bacchae* of Euripides, is a good example of this definition. Most of the essay is an extenuation upon that single point.

What is important to emphasize here, however, is that ritual in my common usage of the term is ceremonial magic, and since my experience with the latter is predicted upon fifty years of association with the Hermetic Order of the Golden Dawn and with Aleister Crowley, it includes or utilizes all the methods and techniques of ceremonial such as are described extensively in this book.

Dr. Israel Regardie
One of the foremost authorities on the theory and practice of Magick.

"...a representative of the great 'occult tradition' of the late 19th century, whose major names include Madame Blavatsky, W.B. Yeats, MacGregor Mathers, A.E. Waite, Aleister Crowley and Dion Fortune. Even in such distinguished company, Regardie stands out as a figure of central importance."–Colin Wilson

At first sight, it may not appear that these methods would be at all necessary in drama. But once it is recognized that all the appurtenances of ceremonial magic are the technical means whereby, on the one hand, considerable power is evoked, and, on the other, the student is exalted to a higher level of consciousness, then it is quite clear that they perform an enormously significant role in ritual, and especially dramatic ritual.

Solely as a preliminary argument, one absolutely essential, to clarify all major issues, it is necessary to indicate that, as the text of the essay points out, the Adeptus Minor Ritual of the Golden Dawn is a perfect example of a dramatic ritual. Whatever may or may not be said about S. L. MacGregor Mathers, it was his genius that gave birth to this ritual. It is of course true that the essentials of that dramatic ritual were borrowed from one of the early Rosicrucian classics, as Ellic Howe has pointed out in his most destructive criticism of the Golden Dawn. But I must hasten to add that Mathers was not under any kind of obligation as a magician or as an artist to borrow anything from the *Fama Fratenatitas* other than what would lend itself to his primary intention–to prepare an initiatory ritual in ceremonial and dramatic form. Without the initiated point of view such as Mathers possessed, nothing of this makes any sense. The non-initiate might just as well leave the whole subject alone, for his or her academic and scholastic viewpoint will only make the subject seem ludicrous–but in the long run make him or her a ridiculous laughing stock.

Apart from Ellic Howe's rather ridiculous book on the Golden Dawn, the most recent example of the futility of unilluminated scholarship is demonstrated by Frances A. Yates in her book *The Rosicrucian Enlightenment*. When discussing this recently with a scholarly friend of mine, he remarked 'But the book is so well documented'. Documented indeed! So well documented that it reminded me of a fantastically amusing satire and parody of the well-documented book in one of Aleister Crowley's earliest writings. It is entitled 'The Excluded Middle or, The Sceptic Refuted' in Volume 1 of his *Collected Works*. It is a dialogue in which almost every word used has a footnote demonstrating not merely the meaning of the word, but giving a pseudo-literary authority for its usage. It is absolutely hilarious. I think Crowley, in the first couple of years of this century, has made an excellent point that is as true to-day as it was then. Scholarship *can* be abused–and is often abused.

For instance, Frances Yates, after an enlightening and revealing survey of some sixteenth- and seventeenth-century history relative to the relationship of the Palatinate kings and the kings of England, prior to the appearance of the three Rosicrucian classics, then remarks:

The story of Christian Rosencreutz and his R.C. Brothers and of the opening of the magic vault containing his tomb was not intended to be taken as literally true by the framer of the manifestoes who were obviously drawing on legends of buried treasures, miraculously rediscovered, such as were particularly prevalent in the alchemical tradition. There is ample evidence in the texts themselves that the story was an allegory or fiction.

Yes–but an allegory of what? Buried treasure as such? Or the rediscovery of the golden treasure in the heart of man which the dramatic ritual–as perceived by the genius of Mathers, and perhaps by some others–was intended to excavate and exalt to the highest.

Yates' prosaic scholarship descends to the totally inane when she remarks 'the opening of the door of the vault symbolizes the opening of a door in Europe'.

The opening of the door of Europe indeed! She recovers sufficiently from her own academic inanity to realize that there *might* be a great deal more–but of this she says very little because, unlike Mathers, she has nothing to say.

Two specific facts of the utmost importance must be kept in mind during the following discussion. The first one is that the Vault of the Adepts, so called, is the essential dramatic focus of the Adeptus, so called, is the essential dramatic focus of the Adeptus Minor Ritual. It is described in full in *The Golden Dawn*. Every year, on Corpus Christi day, this Vault was consecrated anew, with the officiating Adept officer assuming the role of the newly initiated Candidate who is bound to the Cross upon which he pledges himself to his higher and divine Genius. The Consecration of this Vault is none other than the basic ritual described in a half a dozen different ways in this book. It is often referred to as 'Opening by Watchtower'. But by whatever name it is called, it is the means whereby the Vault was consecrated, not to represent the opening of Europe to the Reformation and to the newly developing Science of the Middle Ages, but to the service of the Order to the highest divine possibility of its members and of mankind.

It is imperative to stress this as strongly as I can. The Vault, unconsecrated by the invocation of the higher powers of the Elements as described in an earlier chapter here, is merely a vault, a wooden box, with colours painted on it, a piece of theatrical furniture with no virtue in and for itself. Like a talisman, it is merely an object, worthless and dead–regardless of its beauty and aesthetic value. The function of the Consecrating ceremony is to endow what is dead and worthless with life and vitality and spirit, to give it *meaning*.

The Vault ceremony and the entire Adeptus Minor Ritual are dramatic ceremonies which, like all other dramatic rituals– regardless of how beautiful and moving they may be–need to be blessed and consecrated in one form or another until they become *alive*. Several segments of this essay, as the reader will divine, constantly emphasize that the dramatic ritual described is not unrelated (from the 'meaning' viewpoint) to the Adeptus Minor Ritual. As such the drama is in need of the Consecration and Invocations described at length here.

To sum up briefly, the dramatic ritual, like the Vault ceremony, the Adeptus Minor ceremony, or *The Bacchae*, depends for full theurgic efficacy on the use of all such magical and technical methods which comprise the entire content and tenor of this book. Never let this be forgotten. *The Bacchae* is included in this collection of magical reflections for this very reason.

A Greek Ritual of Magic: The Bacchae

To one intent upon the impartial investigations of religions in order to discern the fundamental unity underlying every religious system and philosophy, a study of one of the great tragedies of Euripides presents a number of luminous parallels and noteworthy ideas of tremendous significance. It is a commonplace long familiar almost to everyone that in nearly all religions there is the oft-recurring legend concerning the divine birth of its greater founder. Or, perhaps, by way of variation, that at least one of the parents was a high divinity. The virgin birth of Jesus Christ for example, whose mother was visited by the Holy Ghost, appears not so extremely dissimilar, where the essential fact is concerned, to that of Dionysus the thyrsus-bearing hero of *The Bacchae*. The myth, so admirably expressed in Gilbert Murray's Notes on *The Bacchae*, informs us that the mother of Dionysus, Semele, being loved by Zeus the Father of all the gods on the holy mount of Olympus, asked her god-like lover to appear to her in the full glory of his splendour. He came, not as did Gabriel to Mary, nor in the form of a pale dove–but as a glittering white blaze of miraculous lightning. So beyond human endurance was this vision, so exalted was she in the ecstasy of this superhuman experience, that Semele died–not before however giving premature birth to a son.

In the gracious poetical form wherein Euripides has enshrined his immortal tragedy, one finds a presaging of the oriental Avatara theory. Within the person of Dionysus there appears to be not simply one personality, one being, but two very definite and distinct personalities. One is more or less mortal, possessed of human frailties and weaknesses; whereas the other is a divine intelligence of superlative wisdom–a God from the topmost heights of the magical mount. Although the names Bacchus and Dionysus are utilized normally to signify one and the same personage who is the central figure of this poetic creation, and are therefore synonymous, yet I wish arbitrarily to differentiate between them for a brief moment in order to demonstrate the existence of the concept of an Avatara. To Dionysus, let us attribute the character of a man–a wise and highly developed or evolved being, in harmony with current theosophical and magical doctrine, one who, having taken destiny into his own hands aeons and aeons ago, by means of a mystical process of spiritual training and interior development, has consciously opened the gates of his being to a transcendental spiritual self, thus obtaining a relative state of human perfection.

Bacchus, on the other hand, could be termed a God in all actuality. Or, if you wish to use the terminology of Jungian psychology, a primordial archetype of the Collective Unconscious. From the theurgic point of view, that could imply a being who, in periods of evolutionary effort long since ended, and thus representing pages torn out from historical record, obtained complete liberation from the cycle of necessity. Transcending all human ties, he becomes one of the hierarchical psychic forces governing some particular aspect of the universe, the sum total of whose intelligence constitutes what we call Nature.

These two beings, Dionysus the man and Bacchus the God, because of certain persisting spiritual affinities, coalesced for a more or less limited period of time, together forming one consciousness, human and divine and cosmic in its scope and significance. The incarnation two thousand years ago at Nazareth was, according to the philosophy of Rudolf Steiner, just such a conjunction of two individualities who, mingling their essences, became known as Jesus Christ.

Shri Krishna of ancient India was another Avatar, as is borne out by the Bhagavad Gita–an incarnation of Vishnu. And the name of Bhagavan Ramakrishna Paramahamsa enjoys also, in some quarters, the reputation of being another and more modern representative of those rare combinations of spirituality and wisdom which incarnate from time to time on this earth for the redemption of mankind.

I believe this hypothesis is amply corroborated by a study of the text itself, which naturally must be the final arbiter of our deductions. In Professor Murray's splendid translation of *The Bacchae* we find, captured by the Theban soldiery, the young and gracious Dionysus confronting boldly and without fear King Pentheus. In this particular statement of the universal myth, Pentheus is comparable in one sense to King Herod of the Jews, and in another sense to Pontius Pilate before whom Jesus was brought to trial. To mocking gibes and taunts of the worst description is the calm Dionysus subjected, as for example when Pentheus throws ridicule on the legendary virgin birth of the God.

> 'Tis all his word,
> This tale of Dionysus; how that same
> Babe that was blasted by the lightning flame
> With his dead mother, for that mother's lie,
> Was re-conceived, born perfect from the thigh
> Of Zeus, and now is God! What call ye these?
> Dreams? Gibes of the unknown wanderer? Blasphemies
> That crave the very gibbet?

The King demands of him the source of his high inspiration–whence came the revelation which has awakened so exuberantly the religious fervour of his people.

> Their intent and use
> Dionysus oped to me, the Child of Zeus.

Spontaneously came this answer. This implies, clearly and indubitably, that although in the text the human being named Dionysus is speaking, yet he refers to another Dionysus, the heavenly child of Zeus who, tentatively, I have denominated Bacchus, the god who inspired the man with light and life and lofty inspiration from above. There would be no real purpose in stating that Dionysus has inspired him, he had not the deliberate intent in mind of differentiating between his own personality and the divine intelligence who dwelt within him.

> Most clear he stood, and scanned
> My soul, and gave his emblems to mind hand.

Thus Dionysus describes the revelation and vision of which he was so recently the recipient. Again, it is quite clear from this that an entity quite apart from his own self is implied. There are two quite distinct entities referred to by Euripides. But Pentheus–the symbol of the conscious ego, of scornful and complacent scepticism, of self-sufficiency and respectability, and representing also the established order of things– consumed with personal pride and violently angry because of the strange rumours rife in his kingdom, remarks that:

> our own
> Wives, our own sisters, from their hearths are flown
> To wild and secret rites; and cluster there
> High on the shadowy hills, with dance and prayer
> To adore this new-made God, this Dionyse…

He is suspicious of this religious revival. Therefore he orders the fair and gentle youth to be enchained. Here we have poetically portrayed the psychological mechanism of repression. The instincts and the vital powers that well up from the primitive unconscious fascinate and yet frighten the ego, the conscious aspect of the psyche. Not understanding the worth and value of the emotional life upon which its own existence rests, and fearful of the dynamic and kinetic quality implicit within the urges which it feels working upon it from without, consciousness instigates a policy of repression and suppression and inhibition. Mocked, reviled, accused of trickery and charlatanism as were all his great predecessors as well as successors, Dionysus is asked whether he actually saw the God and in what form he had appeared.

> What guise
> It liked him. 'Twas not I ordained his shape,

replies Dionysus with subtle confidence, and an underlying contempt for his would-be oppressor. His forehead wreathed with vine tendrils, the broad leaves spreading over his brow, reveals him superficially an effeminate figure, especially with the fawn-skin enveloping his form. As Pentheus first observes:

> Marry, a fair shape for a woman's eye,
> Sir stranger! And thou seek'st no more, I ween!
> Long curls, withal! That shows thou ne'er hast been
> A wrestler!—down on both cheeks so softly tossed
> And winsome! And a white skin! It hath cost
> Thee pains, to please thy damsels with this white
> And red of cheeks that never face the light!

But behind those leaves sharp horns are hidden. And within that delicate and frail-appearing form, despite pale cheeks and curly hair, lurks a mighty spiritual splendour, a fiery will, imperiously demanding absolute obedience. A goo picture of the dynamic and intoxicating quality of the Unconscious.

Perchance it would be a transgression were I to repeat the whole theme at length, particularly when it has already been so perfectly described with such sympathy and insight by Walter Pater in his *Greek Studies*. And moreover, there is the unexcelled text which has been translated with such remarkable fluency and rhythm and beauty by Professor Gilbert Murray. Words indeed cannot adequately describe the eloquence which has been brought to bear upon this translation. It is more upon this translation. It is more than literal translation. Within those pages of the English poetic version Murray has caught the whole of the Dionysian spirit–its overflowing vitality, its intoxication and inspiration–with such a virile spontaneity and luxuriance as to be indicative not so much of mere literal translation but of personal artistic creation. However–a literary criticism of this work is not to be essayed here for that momentous task has already been more than adequately accomplished.

The Bacchae as Magical Ritual

There is another aspect, however, of *The Bacchae* which is seldom expounded by its enthusiasts nor by those devotees of Greek drama who delight in the liquid music of its verse. It is the magical aspect to which I make particular reference. In this mystery play it is certain that a significant magical doctrine of paramount importance is concealed, altogether apart from the theoretical details of a spiritual philosophy. Underlying the play and its theatrical performance is an occult presupposition. In short, experience claims and demonstrates of *The Bacchae* that it may be employed satisfactorily as a magical ritual.

From the magical point of view, the basic purpose and object of ritual and invocation is the calling forth of a God, and the conjoining of the human consciousness with the essence of that God. Psychologically, it may be defined as a means of bringing into the bright light of consciousness the repressed concealed side of the psyche. By means of bringing about an assimilation in consciousness of the vast content of the

Unconscious, the ego is freed from an infantile attitude towards life and from a compulsive bond of union with nature. It becomes able for the first time to sever the unconscious tie of the *participation mystique*. In a word, it is a method of uniting the ego with its own divine essence and root so that man becomes a fully self-conscious individual.

The *Bacchae*, then, is a ceremony, the purport of which is the invocation of that primordial archetype of the Unconscious, that spiritual presence which by the Greeks was denominated Zagreus-Dionysus, Sabazios and Bacchus, but which other peoples in different ages and different climes have conceived of and named in other ways. With the Hindus that praeterhuman presence is named Rama and Krishna and Hari. To the ancient dwellers of the Mediterranean and the inhabitants of hither Asia it was known as Tammuz, Attis, Adonis, Osiris and Mithra, and all the other divinities who, in one way or another, concern the so-called solar myth. The theme of the Asiatic or 'dying' God, which Sir James G. Frazer has so admirably expounded in *The Golden Bough*, is in direct relation with the doctrine at issue. Some years ago, Maurice Maeterlinck excellently epitomized this same concept. 'Dionysus... is Osiris, Krishna, Buddha,' he declares; 'He is all the divine incarnations; he is the god who descends into or rather manifests himself in man; and is death, temporary and illusory, and rebirth, actual and immortal; he is the temporary union with the divine that is but the prelude to the final union...' In *The Bacchae* may be discerned a dramatic ceremony of the same order as, for example, the Third Degree of the Masonic Blue Lodge, the Mass of Catholic Christianity, and the Adeptus Minor Ritual of the but rarely heard of Hermetic Order of the Golden Dawn. To wit, the commemoration and invocation of a god, for the resurrection of man's deeper hidden self from the dark tomb of obscurity and mortality.

The Three Aspects of Ritual

One must lay down, first of all, the preliminary hypothesis that the major operations of Theurgy have not even the remotest connection with the production of curious objective phenomena as some erroneously have supposed; nor with dubious feats of psychism or mediumship. Neither has magic, in this sense, aught to do with what passes today as Spiritualism. The attainment in a mystical rapturous experience of a state of spiritual consciousness is the highest accomplishment of all magical procedure. In the ecstasy of this incomparable experience, known to saints and artists of every age and clime, there is a union of the essence of the microcosm with that greater all-encompassing consciousness which some have variously named God, Spirit, or the Soul of the World.

Now magical ritual possesses three aspects by which this union ensues. The first is a union with a particular deity by means of love, service and devotion. All that which is petty and mean and human is restrained from manifestation; it is a method which may be summarized by the Hindu term *Bhakta*. Here it is necessary to register an emphatic disagreement with Evelyn Underhill. In her work entitled *Mysticism*, Miss Underhill recognizes the fact that will and imagination enter no little into magical work. Yet she is inclined to believe that the Theurgist has but little place for love in his ceremonial operations. This is altogether a false assumption. For how could a god, a being one aspect of whose nature is love itself, be successfully invoked if within the devotee there did not burn a steady flame of the selfsame love? In magical ritual worthy of that name, love must occupy an enormous role.

In the second method, a straightforward simple ceremonial is employed, such as that which figures in the Heptameron of Peter de Abano, the so-called *Goetia* or *The Lesser Key of King Solomon*, and other textbooks of magical instruction and ritual.

By this method, one calls forth from the Astral Light or the Collective Unconscious, with the aid of a trained imaginative faculty and a concentrated will, various of the hierarchies of lesser spiritual beings.

These may legitimately be compared to the constellation of associated ideas or autonomous complexes lurking in the unconscious. With them is locked up a vast store of energy, memory and idea. So long as they are unknown, no evaluation of their worth can be made. Render them accessible to consciousness, however, and, if they can be assimilated, at once you have enriched the psyche, expanded its horizon, and enhanced its nature. By means of their enforced incarnation within the consciousness of the Theurgist, these 'spirits' or archetypes imbue him with the requisite potential of force, thus impelling him in the predetermined direction.

From an analysis of its rituals, there can hardly be imputed a sound metaphysical basis to this method, and its philosophy is extremely crude, to state it mildly. The magician conceives of someone he calls God, upon whom attend a series of angelic beings, variously called archangels, elementals, demons, etc. By simply calling upon this God with a great deal of ado, and commemorating the efforts of previous magicians and saints who accomplished their wonders or attained to the realization of their desires through the invocation of the several names of that God, the magician too realizes the fulfilment of his will. Suggestion obviously must be the decisive factor involved here or, at least, must have a great deal to do with the stirring up of the contents of the Unconscious. It is also the theory that the recital of names, the imaging forth of images and ideas of a certain type, and the projection of the will assisted by the ceremony, has the power of vivifying in the astral light those magical forces of which names and images are symbols. Whatever the real psychological explanation of the way in which this particular technique proceeds, there is little doubt that it works. At least, it works for those who comply with the conditions and have trained themselves in the requisite preliminaries.

The dramatic method is the third and finest aspect, principally for the reason that it combines both the above techniques with the working of a group. Moreover it has the sanction of the highest antiquity. Since it is certainly the method of the poet and in accord with the temperament of all artists, it appears to be the most attractive of all. Its drawback, from one point of view, is that several participants are required, all of whom must sink their personalities in the play and train themselves to work in concert.

On the other hand, there is the equally important fact that a group is enabled to generate a greater supply of energy to provide the basis for a spiritual manifestation than is possible for a single person. In practice, the idea is to arrange a play or a ritualistic ceremony wherein is enacted the entire life-cycle of the God or his terrestrial emissary whose spiritual presence one wishes to invoke. The union or identification with the God is accomplished through suggestion, sympathy and the exaltation of consciousness. For the placing of a keen imagination in harmony with that exemplary life cannot but be a powerful stimulus to the psyche. And what was *once* a fact in nature, the previous ascension of the god into heaven (that is, the occurrence of the mystical experience) may again be repeated on earth. It is not inconceivable that a symbolic or dramatic representation of what was formerly a historical spiritual event in a highly revered personality cannot but assist in a reproduction or a recapitulation of that former union by placing the theurgist in sympathy and magical harmony, through the effect upon his imagination, with the upward trend of the play towards the supreme goal. In fine, the magician *imagines* himself in the ceremony to be the deity who has undergone similar experiences. The rituals serve but to suggest and to render more complete the process of identification, so that sight and hearing and intelligence may serve to that end. In the commemoration, or rehearsal of this history, the magician is uplifted on high, and is whirled into the secret domain of the spirit, there seeing things not lawful to tell to the sons of men.

Loss of Ego-consciousness

While, for the average man, it may be difficult to lose his ego-consciousness in the subject of a play or in a piece of theatrical artistry of any description, for those whose temperament so permits this method is indubitably the most satisfactory.

For instance, in the Adeptus Minor ritual of the Golden Dawn, the initiate watches in the third point of the ritual's progress the resurrection of the Adept Minor ritual of the Golden Dawn, the initiate watches in the third point of the ritual's progress the resurrection of the Adept hierophant from the hidden Pastos or Tomb of Christian Rosenkreutz in the seven sided Vault. Quite unconsciously, he identifies himself through a prodigious effort of will and imagination with the illuminated consciousness of Rosenkreutz, whose medieval adventures are recounted, or with Christ himself, whose mysteries Rosenkreutz attempted to revive. In any event, even if no conscious effort is made apart from aspiring to the higher, an involuntary current of sympathy is aroused which may be sufficient to accomplish the purpose of the ceremony. For the aesthetic appeal to the imagination is almost irresistible.

And the entire action of the dramatic ritual is such that almost despite itself the soul is exalted to the heights, and during that mystical elevation receives the benediction of enlightenment, inspiration and peace. Not always is consciousness of this ecstasy transmitted. There are occasions when several days, weeks, or months are required for the stimulus given to the unconscious aspect of the psyche to penetrate the wall of reserve that has been erected within the Self and produce an effect upon the conscious ego.

Iamblichus, the divine theurgist of Alexandria, speaks of this kind of ritual in *de Mysteriis* as a 'blessed spectacle'. He states that by its means 'the soul acquires another life, energizes according to another energy, and it is then rightly considered as no longer ranking in the order of men. Frequently, likewise, abandoning her own life she exchanges it for the most blessed energy of the Gods'.

With this brief account of the major principles underlying theurgy, let us consider how they may be applied to *The Bacchae* itself. At the very opening of the ceremonial action of this ritual, the principle of Commemoration is employed to awaken through names and ideas the requisite association tracks in the Unconscious, to evoke the primordial archetypes. Before the sacred tomb of his mother, there stands the young adept Dionysus who recounts, in accordance with the principles laid down above, his own history.

> Behold, God's Son is come unto this land
> of Thebes, even I, Dionysus, whom the brand
> of heaven's hot splendour lit to life, when she
> Who bore more, Cadmus' daughter, Semele
> Died here...
>   There by the castle side
> I see her place, the Tomb of the Lightning's Bride.

In the Greek religion of that day, Dionysus was the God of everlasting youth and immortality. He was the genius presiding over the vine, with its correspondence of spiritual inspiration, and the ritual by which he was worshipped was by a kind of apotheosis of intoxication. He is defined by the text:

> He found the liquid shower
> Hid in the grape. He rests man's spirit dim
> From grieving, when the vine exalteth him.
> He giveth sleep to sink the fretful day
> In cool forgetting.

He typifies not only a spiritual principle, but the course of nature as well–her madness, her prodigality and abundance, her supreme joy and vitality. And above all, the god symbolizes her sublime persistence through the mutations of life and death. He is, in a word, a symbol of the spirit itself, that sum total of psychic energy in all its aspects which comprises the nature of man. The play, too, has indirect reference to the dramatisation of spring, when the solar orb comes back to the earth-folk, laden with warmth and light, ripening the wheat and vine in the fields, and bringing to man after the long cold winter the brightness and glory of the Sun. But the Sun was also, among the mystics of every clime, a symbol of certain high aspects of human and divine consciousness, and it was that consciousness which they desired above all to awaken within their hearts.

To suppress, even if but for a moment or two, the ordinary work-a-day consciousness, with its tedium, its inhibitions, its impediment to the expression of the inner self, this was the object of the Dionysiac cult. To supplement it by the plenitude of the all-permanent stream of spiritual life, to submit to the divine power, and effect in consciousness an identification with the sacred essence of Dionysus–such was the intention of the revels of which we have in *The Bacchae* so vivid a description. No stimulus of sense or emotion or mind was omitted to excite and inspire the soul, that the seeds of the new life might manifest from within the dark concealed depths of the psyche.

The purple darkness of night, bright torches illuminating the solitary groves, intoxicating drinks to quieten the mad motion of the brain, orgiastic dances to convulse the limb, making dumb after physical exhaustion the passions and bodily appetites; noble music and inspiring ritual to exalt the soul on high and to exhilarate the spiritual faculties! 'And though the basis clearly enough is physical, yet,' remarks G. Lowes Dickinson, with reference to these mysteries, 'the whole ritual does undoubtedly express that passion to transcend the limitations of human existence.' These are the physical elements of a properly co-ordinated magical ceremony. They are the mnemonic stages so designed as to form a complex though coherent association track as it were, leading the mind from one thing to another towards a divine end.

The ritual's prologue brings us face to face with the magician who, taking the dramatic role of Dionysus, walks by Circe's stream, narrating as in reverie his life-history in such wise as to cause, for the time being, the theurgist to relive in his creative imagination the life of the God–just as, in the Adeptus Minor ritual of the Golden Dawn, the entire history of the movements of Christian Rosenkreutz is narrated. The candidate for initiation hears first of him being sequestered in a monastery, then of his journey eastwards to Damascus, his experiences there, and finally of his return home to Germany with the idea germinating in his mind to formulate an order teaching the knowledge and wisdom he has acquired.

In *The Bacchae* the Chorus of maidens who appear following the departure of Dionysus, fills in the picture to complete for the actors or participants in the rite the details as to whom the god is, and for what spiritual principles he stands. They sing:

> Hither, O fragrant of Tmolus the Golden,
>   Come with the voice of timbrel and drum'
> Let the cry of your joyance uplift and embolden
>   The God of the joy-cry; O Bacchanals, come!
> With pealing of pipes and with Phrygian clamour,
>   On, where the vision of holiness thrills,
> And the music climbs and the maddening glamour,
>   With the wild white maids, to the hills, to the hills!
> Oh, then, like a colt as he runs by a river,
>   A colt by his dam, when the heart of him sings,
> With the keen limbs drawn and the fleet foot a-quiver,
>   Away the Bacchanal springs!

Those celebrants enacting the parts of the intoxicated Maenads–if they have performed aright the imaginative work of formulating vivid images which act as a magnet to the libido stored within the archetypal images in the unconscious, and if they are able to lose personal ego to the suggestion of the play–should likewise experience some faint adumbration of that exuberance and ecstatic frenzy which this song peals for us. For frenzy was a state specially to be cultivated, as being the means whereby the ego submerged itself in a larger fuller life. 'Prophecy cleaves to all frenzy, but beyond all else to frenzy of prayer. Then in us verily dwells the God himself, and speaks the thing to be.' Those who have seen at any time the famous Isadora Duncan, or Anna Pavlova dance her ballet divertissement 'The Bacchanale' will have some fair idea of the orgiastic feelings which this sort of dance can engender.

One of the most noteworthy stage directions indicating the real magical nature of the play, is found where the seer Tieresias is in conversation with the aged father of Semele,

Cadmus. As the first movements of the Bacchic worship commence, he becomes enamoured with its frenzy, excited as though moved by some extraneous agency. 'A mysterious strength and exaltation enter into him.'

Then follows the grand scene of the drama, which is also the climax of the ritual. The gentle exquisite youth, the human Dionysus with his following composed chiefly of Maenads–temporarily deserted by his guiding genius, the divine Bacchus–seems to threaten, at least in the eyes of enthroned authority, the established order of things. That authority, therefore, takes urgent steps, as always it has striven, to put an end to the upstart. Just as, in the instance of Christ, whose opponents claimed that he set himself up against the Roman Empire, Jesus was brought to trial before Pilate to be mocked and scourged and crowned with a wreath of thorns, so likewise was Dionysus. We find him bound and manacled and thrust into the dark dungeon cell, although Pentheus, the inquisitor, is duly warned of the folly of his tyrannical act by his own father and by the seer Tieresias, in which warning occurs the following philosophic strain:

> List and understand,
> King Pentheus! Dream not thou that force is power;
> Nor, if thou hast a thought, and that thought sour
> And sick, oh, dream not thought is wisdom!

Likewise there is the impassioned appeal by a messenger to do no harm to the young god.

> Oh, let him live;
> For if he die, then Love herself is slain,
> And nothing joyous in the world again!

It would be no difficult matter to recast the form of this play to transform it into a magical ceremony, retaining only those sections or verses which actually touch upon the central theme of the dramatic invocation of the God. Several parts or points would need to be devised. Probably one of the most important would need to be that of traditional Magic. All foreign influences would require to be banished from the Temple or scene of the play by means of the proper conjurations, circumambulations and tracings of lineal figures, such as the pentagram and hexagram. This should be followed by a consecration both of the sphere of operation generally, as well as of every person and object within that purified sphere. Incense and holy oils are of supreme importance in this connection. Then, all these preliminary details completed, would follow the act of invoking the forces pertaining generally to the nature of Dionysus, that of the sphere of the Sun, employing a special invocation to be uttered together with the appropriate invoking hexagram ritual. This would complete the first point of the ceremony. The succeeding portions of the play could be a condensed version of this text, retaining the essential features in the most highly dramatic form imaginable.

After the imprisonment of the god, the scene changes to the secrecy of the thickly-wooded groves, where ensues the mysterious worship of Dionysus. To our unaccustomed gaze, Euripides displays a chorus of dancing Bacchantes invoking eagerly and impatiently, with irresistible frenzy and enthusiasm, their beloved deity to visible appearance.

> Lo, we race with death, we perish
> Dionysus, here before thee!
> Dost thou mark us not, nor cherish,
> Who implore thee, and adore thee?
> Hither down Olympus' side,
> Come, O Holy one defied,
> Be thy golden wand uplifted o'er the tyrant in his pride.

Amid earthquakes and thunders–probably the theatrical means of giving actual expression to the sequence of sounds heard psychically as the mystical experience occurs–to the accompaniment of invisible voices issuing from the Castle to announce his appearance, the youthful divinity, now enshrined by his genius, appears and upbraids his maenads for their so little faith in him and his power to escape from tyrannical imprisonment.

> O cast ye, cast ye, to the earth! The Lord
> Cometh against this house! Oh, cast ye down,
> Ye trembling damsels; He, our own adored,
> God's child hath come, and all is overthrown!

To his 'damsels of the Morning Hills', to quote the marvellous description of the Bacchantes, he narrates how, when manacled and bound with chains in the castle dungeons–his guardian genius returned. 'A Voice, and lo, our Lord was come,' says Dionysus. Again, it is necessary to recall the reader's attention to the manner in which Dionysus refers to the 'other' who bears his name also. Without a doubt, the play teachers of two distinct beings acting through one personality.

In dire confusion the shackles fell apart, and the Adept infilled by the presence of his divine lord makes good his release from the prison. Faced by the furious and bewildered Pentheus who utters 'I scorn him and his vines,' Dionysus, now inspired, remarks gently: 'For Dionyse 'tis well; for in they scorn his glory lies.'

He warns the king that in the instigation of repression and persecution he has gone but a step too far, with sage advice suggesting:

> Better to yield him prayer and sacrifice
> Than kick against the pricks since Dionyse
> Is God, and thou but mortal.

Just at this juncture, a king's messenger returns to the castle with almost incredible reports of the bands of the dancing Maenads, of their revels and worship, even of miracles that occurred spontaneously with previous deliberation. He told of strange incidents of girls playing with long quick snakes that hissed and writhed with quivering tongues, of others feeding fawns and young wolf cubs with milk from their own maiden breasts.

> And one would raise
> Her want and smite the rock, and straight a jet
> Of quick bright water came. Another set
> Her thyrsus in the bosomed earth, and there
> Was red wine that the God sent up to her,
> A darkling fountain. And if any lips
> Sought whiter draughts, with dipping finger-tips
> They pressed the sod, and gushing from the ground
> Came springs of milk, And reed-wands ivy-crowned
> Ran with sweet honey, drop by drop.

So it comes about, since the messenger says that if the King had witnessed so holy a scene he would straightaway have gone and worshipped the god, that we approach the secondary crisis of the ritual. The God intimates that perchance Pentheus might wish to see for himself the Dionysian revels celebrated by the Maenads in the fastnesses of the forest groves, and the king, already under the hypnotic spell of the God, acquiesces. That decision is his undoing. Little does he realize that, so intense and unyielding has been his repression, to witness these orgiastic rites can only mean his complete destruction at the hands of an outraged eros. Much to his annoyance, they clothe Pentheus like a Maenad in 'a rich and trailing robe of fine linen', 'a long tress dangling low beneath thy shoulders', the dappled fawn-skin and the ivy thyrsus. Then, with Dionysus accompanying him, he sets out amid secrecy to observe the intoxicating power of the Bacchic revelry.

There is a distinctive psychology of clothing. It is for this reason that magicians everywhere and at all times have employed rich gowns of silk and gorgeously coloured robes. By sympathy, colours and congruous objects may awaken and attract the desired magical forces. It is this important consideration which led certain generations of not highly initiated theurgists to adopt for ceremonial use actual masks, grotesques, and legitimate theatrical artifice. I say not highly initiated advisedly, for it is in the imagination and the imagined inner psychic world where belong these formulated shape and colours of gods and angelic beings. But coloured gowns have an efficacy quite apart from their imagined effect–as demonstrated, in a somewhat similar way, by the use of different coloured rays and lights in therapeutic work.

And while it may be that Euripides causes Pentheus to assume the garb of Maenad solely as disguise in order that his presence may not be divined by the fanatical adherents of the Dionysiac cult, there is nevertheless the significant fact concerning clothing here mentioned which is not often realized. The dappled fawn-skin may quite reasonably represent the chasuble or mantle worn over the fine linen gown which is the magical robe; the tresses and the snood constitute in one sense the nemyss or head-dress, and the ivy thyrsus is his wand. In theurgy, the wand is the symbol of the will–in this case, a sensuous and inhabited animal will, dangerous and prone to explosive moods. Clad like a Bacchante, Pentheus becomes singularly excited, the spirit of the Dionysian frenzy slowly overcoming his otherwise rational behaviour, like some obsessing compulsive emotion welling up from the deeps. He wildly cries:

> What strength is this!
> Kithaeron's steeps and all that in them is–
> How say'st thou–Could my shoulders lift the whole?

And now, too, he obtains a fleeting vision of what Dionysus really is. For whereas the god previously seemed to him a weak and effeminate figure he begins to divine a presence which so far from being feeble and girlish and weak is at once divine and strong and terrible.

> Yea; and mine eye
> Is bright!...
> And is it a Wild Bull this, that walks and waits
> Before me? There are horns upon thy brow!
> What art thou, man or beast? For surely now
> The Bull is on thee!

There are parallels to this sort of vision in the clinical experience of modern psychological work. To a child, it may seem that the feelings and emotions are girlish and effeminate principles of his psyche, not to be encouraged because of fear of ridicule and hurt. Consequently a programme of repression is instigated. No longer are the emotions encouraged and expressed. They are stifled and stilled, until eventually, their evocation in adult life is difficult and tedious. But the psychic life of the individual as expressed in the spontaneous activities of his dream life show the enormous power which these repressed contents of the emotional life really possess. Very often, they produce nightmares and horrible gruesome dreams, in which wild animals–bulls, elephants and tigers, representing the cruelly inhibited feelings, play a very active part.

Once again, the point of the ritual closes, and Euripides shifts the scene of the tragedy. The practising theurgists are replunged headlong into the dance of the Maenads who chant their magical invocations. I quote two verses in particular, since these few lines correspond, more so perhaps than any others in the entire play, with conjurations have been couched. The first occurs quite early in the ritual, the second comes much later on.

Up, O Bacchae, wife and maiden,
  Come, O ye Bacchae, come;
O bring the joy bestower,
God-seed of God the Sower,
Bring Bromios in his power
  From Phrygia's mountain dome;
To street and town and tower,
  Oh, bring ye Bromios home!

Appear, appear, whatso thy shape or name
  O Mountain Bull, Snake of the Hundred Heads,
  Lion of Burning Flame!
O God, Beast, Mystery, come! Thy mystic maids
Are hunted!–Blast their hunter with thy breath,
  Cast over his head thy snare;
And laugh aloud and drag him to his death,
Who stalks thy herded madness in its lair!

Again Euripides has recourse to a technicality of stagecraft whereby to convey the death of King Pentheus, thus rendering the dramatic efforts of the magical participants less arduous. A messenger, pale and distraught, enters hastily from the mountains. Bearing the news to the leader of the Chorus, he tells how Pentheus had gone to Kithaeron's slopes with Dionysus to watch while in ambush the mode of Dionysian worship. There the king had been captured by the Maenads, enraged at one spying upon their secret worship. Spurred on by Agave, his own mother–who, however, enraptured by the Bacchic ecstasy knew not what she did, nor did she recognize the royal person of their victim–Pentheus was torn limb from limb by the Bacchantes. As the climax after the tragedy of the death of the principal enemy of the God, there follows then the ascension of Dionysus to heaven upon a cloud–symbolic of spiritual triumph and illumination.

The Solar Significance of The Bacchae

Thus *The Bacchae* ends–upon a lyrical note of magical exaltation. It is an epic, theurgic, religious and philosophic in implication, depicting the triumph and victory of the God over his oppressors. It is therefore a divine history most suitable for ceremonial presentation.

The whole drama is solar in significance. Yet not only astronomically so, but spiritually. In every system of religious philosophy, the Sun represents the symbol of all that is highest, finest, and best in man. Not only is the Sun our father and redeemer even from a physical point of view, but the whole of our inner spiritual existence, which is the real life of us, is ultimately bound up in all sorts of ways with that of the sun. As we see it, the Sun is the outer vehicle of the inner spiritual sun; the flaming garment of a God or a hierarchy of gods, of whose nature we are part and parcel. They dwell in us, and we in them, and from their supernal existence we may not be separated even for one instant of time.

The student of ancient religions will have noted the indubitable fact that the great teachers of Magic almost without exception identified with the cycle of the Sun's eternal journey through the heavens. Or rather, to be somewhat more accurate, the cycle of their individual lives attached itself to the greater cycle of the sun. The Nativity at the Winter Solstice and the Crucifixion at the Vernal Equinox are quite obvious in suggesting the birth of the Saviour and his elevation above the order of physical matter. The Autumnal Equinox, just prior to the going down of the sun to its hiding for the long dark winter, may also suggest to a keen imagination, as it did to the worshippers of Mithra and Dionysus, the obscuration of the Sun and the imprisonment of the God in a dungeon. There are numerous variations upon this one central theme, but the symbols are nearly always equivalent.

Yet since the Sun does simultaneously represent a spiritual value, the theurgists of all time have endeavoured to utilize the recurrence of this divine force for the illumination and advancement of mankind. The methods varied, depending entirely upon the temperament of the people to whom they were endeavouring to pass on their message, and the intelligence of the immediate individuals with whom personally they had magical commerce. In *The Bacchae* of Euripides we may perceive another attempt, and a very fine one indeed, to drive home to the Greeks through the medium of the theatre and by way of tragedy, the same old lesson, the identical teaching which was given to all antiquity.

Symbolism in The Bacchae

The symbolism is far from difficult to trace. Psychologically, it is very descriptive indeed. One may almost detect the entire mechanism of the Freudian scheme there–from repression and resistance right up, or down, to the Oedipus complex. Pentheus in the ritual is the dramatic representation of ordinary consciousness–that personal egoic faculty which wilfully blinds itself to the limitations of its own power, and to the existence of other powers even within its own household. Since it falsely believes as a matter of habit that it and it alone is the supreme power, and that all else matters not at all, this source of power must be deliberately sacrificed on the mystic altar before illumination can take place. This personal ego endeavours ruthlessly to repress both the divine spirit which is its lord and creator, as well as the natural instincts, of which latter the Maenads, wild, hysterical, and mad that they were, furnish a most apt symbol. If the instincts are too violently repressed, then because of the clogging of the personal unconscious, and because of the explosive tendency which the unconscious develops, consciousness becomes narrow and delimited, and quite unable to receive inspiration and energy from the Collective Unconscious. In the Jungian analysis, it becomes necessary first to analyse away, so to speak, the repressed instincts that have been thrust out of sight. By rendering them accessible to consciousness, it then becomes possible to deal adequately with the Collective Unconscious which was quite distant from treatment before.

This rational consciousness of man, represented in the drama by King Pentheus, in overstepping the legitimate confines of its power and proper activity, is torn into mere shreds of bleeding flesh by those archaic forces he seeks erroneously to repress and thrust out from his kingdom–where, and only where, they truly belong. His own mother, typifying here the inchoate destructive aspect of Nature, being the first to claw at his throat. Psycho-analysis is wealthy with lurid details and innumerable cases of those misguided individuals whose integrity of consciousness has been torn asunder by the repressed unconscious forces of their being. And it almost seems as if Euripides presages–or else had a deep intuitive insight into–the Freudian concept of the passionate mother effect which first of all brings into existence the repression mechanism. It is this repressed mother fixation, around which all subsequent repressed material and emotion constellates by association, that in the long run proves to be the undoing of the unenlightened individual by ruining all his attempts toward social adaptation and the leading of a normally useful life. How profoundly has not Euripides depicted the revenge of the terrible Mother!

Both the King and the Maenads–both ego-consciousness and the instinctual urges– have their rightful place in the scheme of things, each has its respective place in the universe. For the one to usurp or interfere with the true functions of the other is at once to invite chaos and complete disorganization.

Bacchus-Dionysus represents the vital stream of spiritual energy, the totality of man's forces. He represents the Sun in its dual aspect, particularly the symbol of the central intoxicating and ecstatic spirit to be invoked into human consciousness during the ineffable rites. To his services must the Maenads be dedicated. For he is the life of the instincts, that which motivates and directs their movement. Nor should Pentheus interfere with the divinity's true progress, for he can have no notion of the true import and significance of the intentions, teleological and immediate, of the god. Let him not interfere, so that the abounding vitality and never-to-be-exhausted intoxication of the God may freely be shed upon all and sundry.

His ceremonial imprisonment and manacling may refer to two phenomena. One the loss of spirit, with the consequent neurasthenia, experienced by the neurotic when repression has proceeded too far. And on a higher level of interpretation, to the obscuration of the spiritual self during the 'dark night of the soul'. Only the return of the sun, or the magical descent of the God into the mind, can lift that black night of horror and despair. The self-devised release from prison, with the subsequent death of the tyrant oppressor, likewise has at least two planes of interpretation.

It can quite easily refer to the effect of schizophrenia–the complete splitting of consciousness, and the loss of integrity and sanity–the destruction of King Pentheus. Moreover, in a far deeper sense, it represents the successful appearance of the invoked force and its incarnation within the inmost hearts of its devotees, banishing forever enslavement to the world's complacent and hypocritical attitude towards life and living. On the physical plane, the oncoming of Spring in all its glory for the frucification of all life is seen here, the eternal sanctification and spiritual consecration of every being to that inspiring miracle which year after year proceeds without diminishment and without abatement.

The rehearsal of this tragic history of Euripides' *The Bacchae* implies to the company of theurgists all these doctrines, and exalts the human consciousness beyond its normal bounds and confines. At the same time, by means of the magical invocations, the power of sound applied to the vibration of the Names, and the actual assumption of the astral God-form, the God himself may be called forth, and with his divine essence the company conjoin themselves in bliss.

And the result of this Magic is an acceleration of the development of the Spirit. Whereas long countless ages are required for the evolution and growth of the mass of mankind towards a distant ideal of spiritual perfection, the Magician seeks to further his progress, and to evolve more rapidly to that goal which ultimately must be reached by all. 'The outcome of the telestic union with the Gods is an improvement of every faculty and power of mind in the constitution of man. For the Gods, or the universal essences of light to theurgists in unenvying abundance, call upwards their soul to themselves, procuring them a union with themselves, and accustoming them, while they are yet in a body, to be separated from bodies, and to be led round to their eternal and intelligible principle.'

Robert Anton Wilson

THE DREAM ILLUMINATI
A Global Revolution Takes Wing

*Introduction by
Robert Anton Wilson, Ph.D.*

This book concerns dreams of flight, and the achievement of flight. Historically, dreams of flying appeared in the collective unconscious before the reality of flight existed in technology, and it seems plausible that if we understood our dreams better we would use our technology more wisely. Our machines manifest our dreams in matter crafted to coherence, and a psychoanalysis of our culture could easily derive from an examination of how we use science to materialize our fantasies and nightmares.

Why have we always dreamed of flying, and why have we built flying machines? This question seems "eminently" worth pondering in a world where 200,000,000 people pass through Kennedy International Airport every year, flying the Atlantic in one direction or the other.

To understand the profound, it often appears helpful to begin with the clues that seem trivial. I suggest that we contemplate what our children look at every Saturday morning on TV. One of the most popular jokes in animated cartoons shows the protagonist walking off a cliff, without noticing what he has done. Sublimely ignorant, he continues to walk–*on air*–until he notices that he has been doing the "impossible" and then he falls. I doubt very much that there will be any reader of this book who has not seen that routine at least once; most of us have seen it a few hundred times.

It might seem pretention to see a Jungian archetype adumbrated in crude form in this Hollywood cliché, but follow me for a moment.

When Hollywood wishes to offer us the overtly mythic, it presents Superman, who can "leap over tall buildings in a single bound," and a more recent hero named *Luke Skywalker*.

The Tarot, that condensed encyclopedia of the collective unconscious, begins with the card called The Fool, and the Fool is depicted walking off a cliff–just like Donald Duck or Wily Coyote in the cartoons.

A Greek legend (which James Joyce took as the archetype of the life of the artist) tells us of Daedalus and Icarus: Daedalus who, imprisoned in a labyrinth (conventional "reality"), invented wings and flew away, over the heads of his persecutors, and Icarus, the son of Daedalus, who flew too close to the Sun Absolute and fell back to Earth. Like Porky Pig walking off a cliff; Icarus's fall contains a symbolism many have encountered in their own dreams.

The Sufi order employs as its emblem a heart *with wings* (and the Ordo Templi Orientis employs a circle–symbolizing both emptiness and completion–*with wings*). The Egyptian god of wisdom, Thoth, had the head of a winged creature, the ibis; his Greek equivalent, Hermes, was portrayed as more human, but had bird's wings on his sandals.

The Wright Brothers, who made flying possible for all of us, remain beloved figures in the folk imagination–but how many readers can name the inventors of such equally marvelous (but Earthbound) devices as the television, the vacuum cleaner, the computer, the laser or the modern indoor toilet? Yet while other geniuses seem "forgotten by the masses," the classic put-down to satirize any conservative who sets limits to what human art can accomplish remains "I told Wilber and I told Orville, you'll never get that crate off the ground."

I suspect that part of the function of flight consists in destroying our concept of limit; opening us to the insight Dr. John Lilly expressed so eloquently in *The Center of the Cyclone:* In the province of the mind, what is believed to be true is true or becomes true, within limits to be found experimentally and experientially. These limits are further beliefs to be transcended. I the province of the mind, there are no limits.

The poet Hart Crane, trying to describe what Wilbur and Orville meant to his generation (he died in the 1930s), wrote that from Kitty Hawk onward, he sensed "the closer clasp of Mars." By 1938 people tuning in on an Orson Welles radio program after the drama started *believing* they were hearing a newscast and that the Martians were already here. A quantum jump had occurred in the limits of our social imagination. Humanity had, like the poet, sensed the "closer clasp" of Mars.

Just slightly more than 30 years later, Neil Armstrong walked on the moon, like a character in the fiction of Jules Verne, and ten years later, our instruments invaded the Martian desert already familiar to "us" through the visions of Edgar Rice

Burroughs and Ray Bradbury. If this does not confirm William Blake's notorious claim that "poetic Imagination" should be considered another name for "God", it certainly suggests that Poetic Imagination may function as another name for Destiny.

Perhaps we should ponder more deeply on the fact that Daedalus means "artist" in Greek. Daedalus, designer of labyrinths, imprisoned by those he served, in a labyrinth he himself built–Daedalus, inventor of wings that took him from the Earth to Outer Space–why does he represent Art, instead of Science?

Well, to understand this we must remember that the ancient Greeks did not distinguish Art and Science as we do. The genius of an artist, Aristotle says, lies in his *tekne*, the root from which we get our word, "technology"; but *tekne* basically means sill or craft, or the ability to make things that never existed before.

In our age, by contrast, Stravinsky was regarded as "witty" or "paradoxical" (or deliberately enigmatic) when he called himself a "sound engineer". An artist who considers himself a kind of engineer? That is a hard thought for us to grasp. Yet, a few moments reflection will show that as much precise structural knowledge can be found in Stravinsky's music as in Roebling's blueprints for the Brooklyn Bridge–that edifice (considered "miraculous" when it was new) which Hart Crane took as a symbol of the unity of Art and Science.

Our dichotomized and dualistic thinking has been denounced so often lately that I hardly need labor this point. I would prefer to suggest a possible common origin of both art and science. The musician and the architect, the poet and the physicist, I propose, may be best considered late evolutionary developments of the type that first appears as the shaman–and shamans in most cultures are known as "they who walk in the sky," just like the latter day shaman-hero, Luke Skywalker.

It should not be regarded as accidental or arbitrary that Swift put Laputa, the home of scientists, in the sky, in order to disparage science for not having all four feet on the ground; Aristophanes put Socrates in the clouds to similarly disparage philosophy. Outer Space seems the natural home of all descendents of the shaman, whether they be called artists, philosophers or scientists.

The ironies of Swift and Aristophanes, and the myths of the fall of Icarus and Wily Coyote, indicate that the collective unconscious contains a force opposed to our dreams of flight. This appears inevitable. As Jung, the foremost explorer of the collective psyche, often pointed out, an ineluctable polarity exists in the symbols of dream and myth, a "Law of Opposites" which Jung compared to the Chinese concept of yin and yang energies. Jekyll contains Hyde; love easily becomes hate; Cupid and Psyche reappear as the Phantom of the Opera and Margaritta, and also as King Kong and Fay Wray.

In the present context, the Law of Opposites means that we yearn to soar, yet we fear to fall. Our "inner selves" are mirrored not just in Orville Wright rising like a bird from Kill Devils Hill at Kitty Hawk, but also in Simon Newcombe, the great astronomer, who "proved" mathematically that such flight was impossible.

As I have elsewhere suggested, *neophilia* and *neophobia*–love of novelty and fear of novelty–result from the primal polarities of the first imprint of the newborn infant. In other words, what Dr. Timothy Leary calls the bio-survival system, I prefer to call it, since it includes the immune, endocrine and neuropeptide sub-systems as well as the autonomic nervous system–imprints either basic explorativeness or basic conservatism very quickly. That explains, I think, why some babies "chortle with delight" when tossed up in the air and caught, while others scream with terror. Infants who like this experience of flight, I suggest, already have the neophiliac imprint and those who act terrified have the neophobic imprint.

Of course, "the universe" can count above two (even if Aristotelian logicians cannot) and few of us are either pure neophiliacs or pure neophobics. Rather, we wobble about on a gradient between neophilia and nephobia–between joy and anxiety, between conservatism and experimentalism, between yearning to soar and the fear of falling. At times we feel like Jonathan Livingston Seagull, convinced that *"a true Heaven has no limits"* and trying to fly higher and faster; other times we become the old Reaganite gulls, nervously warning that to fly too high too fast will ruin your brain and directly contradicts the traditional mores of the flock ("Just say *no* to soaring").

We contain both Orville Wright leaping into the air toward a future "where no man has gone before" and Simon Newcombe proving that Orville will certainly fall and smash himself like Humpty Dumpty.

As Joyce so poetically writes:

> *My great blue bedroom, the air so quiet, scarce a cloud. In peace and silence. I could have stayed up there for always only. It's something fails us. First we feel. Then we fall... If I seen him come down on me now under whitespread wings like he'd come from Arkangels, I sink I'd die down under his feet, humbly, dumbly, only to washup.*

Despite the multiple dream-images here–the Irish rain falling to become the Irish river Anna Liffey, Lucifer and his hosts falling from Heaven, the falls of Adam and Eve and Humpty Dumpty, Mary receiving the divine seed from the Archangel, Magdalen washing the feet of the Saviour, the paraclete descending as a dove to bring the Apostles the Gift of Tongues, a housewife washing up the breakfast dishes–Joyce primarily invokes our deep awareness that gravity "pulls us down," as well as our deep yearning to break free of this "drag" and to soar back to our home above the clouds.

In 1988, the ancient Egyptian and Gnostic belief that our origin and our destiny reach far beyond Earth no longer seems as quaint and queer as it did in recent generations. In books like Dr. Timothy Leary's *Info-Psychology*, Dr. Francis Crick's *Cosmic Panspermia* and Sir Fred Hoyle's *Evolution from Space*, there appears a body of evidence strongly suggesting that life did not begin on this planet but arrived here from elsewhere in space. While the interpretations of these brilliant philosopher-scientists differ–Leary thinks life was planted here by advanced intelligences lovingly seeking "children" for companionship, while Crick proposes that advanced civilization created Earth-side DNA as an interesting experiment, and Hoyle argues that some seeds go here by accident (on comets, etc.) and some was deposited by Higher Intelligences for reasons inscrutable to us at present–their various kinds of evidence, from diverse fields of enquiry, does make a strong case that evolution is older and more universal than we traditionally think. One leaves their books suspecting that the orthodox biological view regarding Early evolution apart from Cosmic evolution results from unvoiced pre-Copernican assumptions about Earth's centrality and its isolation.

In addition to the sophisticated and learned works of Leary, Crick and Hoyle, we have also recently witnessed the growth of a vast body of "vulgar" or at least popular literature arguing the proposition that Ancient Astronauts seeded this planet, not with all life, but merely with (post-Neanderthal) humanity. Instead of dissecting the flaws in the arguments of this seemingly "crank" literature, it might be more illuminating, I think, to wonder why this popular mythos provides the masses with an unsophisticated and anthropocentric form of the theories more soberly presented in works like *Info-Psychology, Cosmic Panspermia,* and *Evolution from Space.* Why do we find both first-rate and second-rate minds suddenly preoccupied with extraterrestrial evolution, while ninth rate minds increasingly embrace Pop UFOlogy?

And why, one may next wonder, does this theme also appear centrally in the most beautiful, the most "haunting" and the most often-revived science-fiction film of all time–Kubrick's magnificent *2001*?

When one idea or archetype appears in learned tomes, in tabloids, in folk-belief, in new cults, and in great art, all at about the same time, one suspects the presence of what Jung called, in his book *Flying Saucers*, "a shift in the constellation of the archetypes." In terms of current neuroscience, what Jung means, I think, is that the DNA/CNS "dialogue"–the neuropeptide "language" between genes and brain–is preparing us for a new evolutionary leap.

Later in this book, you will read a scene in which the hero says bluntly:

"I realized that I was only as free as I thought myself to be and that there is no limit to how high we can fly!"

Here we see again that the archetype of flight always carries an umbilical connection to the idea of the transcendence of all limits. ("What is believed to be true is true or becomes true...")

And we must wonder again if more than childish fantasy lurks in the concept of Wily Coyote walking on air only until he "remembers" that this "is" officially "impossible" in our current reality-tunnel.

In 1904, when Einstein was starting to write his first paper on Relativity and the Wright Brothers were testing the airplane design that finally worked after many failures, Aleister Crowley, the most controversial mystic of our century, "received"–or created by Poetic Imagination–a document which he ever after believed was a communication from Higher Intelligence. In this work, called *Liber AL* or *The Book of the Law*, there is contained what purports to be a message from "Nuit," the Egyptian star goddess, interpreted in Crowley's commentaries as the supreme consciousness of the cosmos, or the sum total of all synergistically interactive intelligences throughout space-time. Among other things this "entity" or corporation told Crowley

Every man and every woman is a star...
I am above you and in you. My ecstasy is in yours.
My joy is to see your joy.
For I am divided for love's sake, for the chance of union...
Put on the wings, and arouse the coiled splendor within you: come unto me!

Many interpretations of these verses are possible; you may be astonished later, in fact, as some possible meanings that are not at all clear now will be strongly present if you gaze back at this page after finishing the novel before you.

Personally, after reading some of the current scientists who see evolution as both terrestrial and extraterrestrial, I cannot look at the words of *Liber Al* without thinking that, in some sense, the interstellar creators who planted life here may be sending us a signal to return to our home in the stars–that "great blue bedroom" which Joyce poetically invokes on the last page of *Finnegans Wake* and in which the astronaut, David Bowman, abruptly finds himself at the climax of *2001*.

Of course, the language of poetic myth, like that of dream, should always be considered analogical and allegorical, not literal; to see only one meaning here (or in the novel to come) means that one will "fall down into the pit called Because, and there he shall perish with the dogs of Reason" (to cite Crowley again). The content of a true archetype contains an infinity of mirrors.

For instance, my Dream Diary for 23 April 1968 records that when I woke in the morning I remembered the following images from my night's hermetic journey:

> 1. I am in a Chicago nightclub once patronized by John Dillinger. I find that the present patrons are also a group of gangsters. They regard me with hostility and I become frightened. I try to leave; they try to stop me. I open a door.
> 2. I find myself on the IRT subway in New York. I am riding in the front car and watching the tunnel ahead of the train (as I did as a boy). Suddenly, I see a brick wall ahead and realize the train is going to crash into it and kill everybody aboard, including me.
> 3. I am out of the subway and walking in Cicero, Illinois. An angry mob surrounds me. They seem to know that I was in the recent Martin Luther King march against segregation here. I cannot escape them. Suddenly, I know intuitively what to do. I cry out, "Elohim!" and sprout wings and fly above their heads. The sky is beautiful and I feel free of all anxieties, at peace, unreasonably hopeful about everything.

When I awoke, I was thinking of Chesterton's description of the mystic experience as "absurd good news."

At the time of this dream, I was involved with Chicago friends in propagating the John Dillinger Died For You Society, a parody of Fundamentalist religions which, like all good jokes, had its serious side. I was fascinated by the way that certain outlaws like Dillinger (or Jesse James, or Robin Hood) were virtually forced to live to the full archetypal myth of Osiris, Dionysus, Adonis, Christ–and Joyce's Tim Finnegan. I also meditated much on the way in which outlaws who did not even approximately "live" the myth subsequently had their lives rewritten in folk-imagination to conform to it. The first part of the dream-record confronts me with the dark side of the archetype, and reminds me that real gangsters are not the mythic figures imposed on them by Poetic Imagination but nasty and frightening sociopaths.

In the second part of the dream, I enter into the Underground Initiation. Although using symbols from my own life (the subway), I find myself retracing the steps of Ishtar in the land of the dead, Odysseus sailing to Hades for wisdom, Jesus and Dante descending to Hell, etc. In alchemy this was called the *negrito*, which Jung compares to the initial stages of psychotherapy.

In a sense, the Underworld Journey appears the reciprocal of, and preparation for, the Achievement of Flight. Dante had to walk through Hell before climbing Mount Purgatory and soaring above the clouds of Heaven. In retrospect, I am especially delighted with the Freudian wit of the unconscious in using modern "Underworld" figures–gangsters–to represent the mythic Underworld.

In the third part of the dream, the traditional Wrathful Demons attack me, personified by the citizens of Al Capone's hometown, Cicero, perhaps because the people out there always reminded me of Wrathful Demons whenever I had to associate with them. I escape by crying out a name of the Hebrew Bible, whereupon I am able to fly, like Dante or Daedalus, from the Pit of the Stars.

What I find most curious about these dream fragments is that, when I experienced them in 1968, I knew nothing about Cabala. I was puzzled on awakening about the name *Elohim* and the way I had magically used it in the dream. All I knew about that name in those days was that it appears in the first chapter of Genesis and that there is a dispute between the philologists and theologians about whether it means "God" or "the gods"–i.e. whether the first chapter of the Bible is or isn't a fragment left over from a polytheistic phase of Judaism.

It was over two years after this very Jungian dream that I became interested in Cabala and eventually learned that *Elohim* is therein considered a great Name of Power–used in e.g. the Middle Pillar Ritual, which every Cabalist in training is expected to do at least once a week. The function of Cabalistic ritual in general, and this ritual in particular, was once defined by Crowley as "to raise the mind of the student perpendicularly to Infinity"–beyond all limits. This is symbolized in my dream, as in many dreams and myths, by the imagery of flight and the conquest of gravity. The 1968 dream seems to contain precognition of Cabalistic work I would be doing very seriously c. 1971-75.

Of course, if one dares to suggest that a dream contains precognition, the Rationalist immediately declares the connection between the dream image and later waking events as "mere coincidence." The "coincidence" becomes more provocative, however, when one considers that my interest in Cabala was aroused by the books of Israel Regardie, and this present novel is being published by Dr. Christopher S. Hyatt, a former student of Regardie's. Both Dr. Hyatt and Dr. Regardie have been Jungian therapists, and it was Jung who inspired me to keep a dream diary and look for "coincidences" between the dream-world and the awake-world. These links (Wilson-Regardie-Hyatt–the

1968 dream-my later study of Cabala-the present novel) seem to suit Jung's definition of synchronicity as "psycho-logically induced space-time relativity."

At the time I had this dream or set of dreams in 1968, I was suffering from a moderately severe depression and the general symptoms of what is now called "mid-life crisis." I had a very good job at Playboy magazine, with an excellent salary for the 60s, but I was approaching 40 and wanted to write full-time. (Three years later, after beginning Cabalistic work, I quit my job and have been writing full-time ever since. Although I experienced the usual share of shocks, disappointments and bereavements, I have not suffered clinical depression again.)

The reader might find it illuminating to compare this record with a dream recounted in Joseph Campbell's *The Hero With a Thousand Faces*. In this case, the dreamer saw a winged horse with one wing broken, struggling to fly and falling continually back to Earth. Campbell does not ever bother interpreting this symbolism, merely informing us that the dreamer was a poet forced to work at a menial job to support his family; one understands immediately.

In a sense, we have all had our "wings" broken; it remains the major function of such "hallowed institutions" as organized religion and free compulsory education to see that our "wings" are broken, or at least clipped, before we reach adulthood. How else will society have the insectoid units it needs to fill the cubicles in its hive economy?

But what if we begin to regrow healthy organs of Poetic Imagination and flight? What if we "put on the wings and arouse the coiled serpent within" as *Liber AL* urges? Is it not predictable that society will react with all the fury described by Wayne Saalman in this novel? Joyce did not name his emblematic Artist merely Daedalus, Stephen Dedalus–after St. Stephen Proto-martyr who reported a Vision and was stoned to death for it.

And does it not appear ultimately beneficial, in evolutionary perspective, that society should react in that manner? Those of us who have no avocation for martyrdom must learn, when we realize how much neophobia remains built into the contraptions of "society" and "the State," the art of surviving in spite of them. In a word, we must "get wise" in both the Socratic meaning of that phrase and in the most hardboiled street meaning. Neophobia functions as an Evolutionary Driver, forcing the neophiliac to get very shrewd very fast, just as stupidity provokes the merely intelligent to become also clever and cunning.

For the rest, I thin this novel speaks very eloquently for itself–to those who are ready to read between the lines. As a final bit of gnomix exegesis, I offer you Proposition 12 of Aleister Crowley's masterwork, *Magick*:

> *Man is ignorant of the nature of his own being and powers. Even his idea of his limitations is based on experience of the past, and every step in his progress extends his empire. There is therefore no reason to assign theoretical limits to what he may be, or to what he may do.*

Excerpt from:
CRUMBS...And Other Things I've Followed Home
Jeff Mandon

We really see in spiritual work, that progress is not a straight line. Invariably we find ourselves enacting the same old behavior. The shift occurs when we find ourselves in the same circumstances or enacting the same behavior but with a new awareness. So, we use that awareness to interrupt the pattern and reroute; to literally change everything. Some may think this is an act of rebellion; and perhaps it is, but it is a necessary one. A natural one. At some point our growth depends on our casting off the constraints and spiritual shackles of a regimented society based on an egoistic value system where humanity is secondary to short-term economic gain. And like it or not we

Sculpture by Jeff Mandon

get sucked into this value system and fuel it, unless we at some point confront it squarely and pass ourselves to redefine our needs and wants based on our heart's desire; not our head's. We try to honor our authentic Self.

Heads up. God is not Santa Claus. Instead of demanding that God bring us the red bike we wanted or the red Maserati we wanted, or whatever else we desire so ardently at a particular moment, we take a breath, gather our maturity, and instead affirm that whatever would make us truly happy is manifesting in our lives now. Ask for the awareness and discernment to recognize God's gifts to us. We ask for the clarity and the ability to respond to God's guidance, day by day, moment by moment.

We trust.

We doubt.

We ask for help even in this, and we renew our trust with greater conviction. We may even ramble off all of our fears and doubts and hopes and desires and whatever we need to do to release ourselves from the notion that our happiness rests solely on the fulfillment of this particular thing or circumstance for which we're praying. And no matter how much we may be feeling that if this particular relationship, or job, or healing does not take place all is lost, we remind ourselves that God is abundant and therefore given we are His children, so are we. We seek to broaden our scope and increase our trust and to release ourselves of the knee-jerk fear response of clutch and grab and "tunnel vision".

We keep breathing. We remind ourselves that like attracts like, and where we place/contribute our focus is a vote for more of the same. With those two principles in tow, we remind ourselves also, that our happiness depends not only on our working to get what we want, but working equally hard at wanting what we get. This is not wordplay or a trivial exercise. It is an essential exercise in gratitude, backed up by the principles I've just mentioned. As best we can, we try to focus on that which we are thankful for in our lives. Being grateful for what you don't have, such as "I'm grateful I don't have terminal cancer" is not the same thing. Even if it's a short and petty list, we take it now.

We list only that for which we genuinely feel grateful; and while we consider these things, we do our best to fully embrace gratitude. We notice its qualities—how it feels, sounds, how it shifts our body inside, and our mind. And while we do so, we remain open to expanding our list as other things come to mind. We don't force this and we don't berate ourselves, and nobody has to know the length of our list and what's on it at any given moment.

The reason that this is important is that it allows us a window through which we make an energetic shift. I mentioned the phenomenon whereby we get fixated. We get something in our sites and we're looking to bag it because we've decided this and only this, will make us happy. Some people surely have already learned the skinny on this point, but for me and most of the people I've spoken with, this lesson crops up at some point along the path.

For me, it manifested as an attachment to a particular relationship in my 30s. I thought this was just it, the be all, end all relationship for me. When it ended, I could not foresee ever wanting to be romantically involved with anyone else, and eventually worked myself into a state where some sick part of me was bound and determined that I would not be happy without this come hell or high water.

I held myself emotionally hostage, and the ransom note listed this particular form of this particular relationship...or else. It was an unholy mess; and all these years later, still a bit of a sore spot; embarrassing, to say the least. What I noticed was that at some point I kept expecting my will to survive to kick in, and I would pull up out of this downward spiral. It didn't really happen as clearly as that, but what I did notice was that when I let go of the idea that my happiness or survival depended on that relationship, I would slowly start to pull up and return to sanity. The trouble was that I would get better, and start to pull myself together again, and then at a certain point I would feel that now I was doing better I should return my attention to the task of renewing this relationship. It was a textbook case of when that which is intoxicating becomes toxic.

So, lo and behold as soon as I'd initiate contact with my former lover, down I'd go again. I was praying my guts out—at first for the return of this relationship, then finally the willingness to release it, though I was unwilling to do just that; and I'd continue to sink and degrade. As you can imagine, I was one big ball of desperation. And we all know how attractive that is. And I couldn't understand why it was happening—that's how thick my delusion was. I was certain God and I were nearing an agreement, and he'd seen the error of his ways. And it wasn't that I was closed to his input, but merely that in this instance I was right, He was wrong, there was no two ways about it, and why the hell did he let us get involved only for the relationship to fail? What kind of loving God would do that?! Hunh?! Right?!! Hunh?!

As far as I was concerned, God owed me and he owed me big for this one. Talk about betrayal. Between my ex and God, betrayal and I not only made each other's acquaintance, but were inseparable for months. What made matters worse was that I was meditating and using every tool at my disposal to hear spirit and I simply couldn't receive messages. At least I couldn't receive them by the means to which I'd grown accustom. It freaked me out. They say that our egos (in whatever guise they adopt) are cunning, baffling, powerful, and patient. I would add from my experience that if we think our ego has grown strangely quiet or perhaps has gone off for a while; it may have, but trust that wherever it is it is plotting...and doing push-ups. Lucky for me as cunning, baffling, powerful, and patient as ego is, God is even more so. Since he couldn't get through to me one way, he decided to go for another.

By this time, I'd been up and down so often my coping strategy consisted of chain-smoking, alienating everyone, ordering out for food, sobbing at the drop of a hat, and in moments of particular pain, throwing up my arms and shrieking. I mean, I figured if I was going to be on a rollercoaster I may as well act like it. So I had the tube on, and I had taken a break from crying and chain-smoking...well, not from the chain-smoking, but from crying, and I was watching a documentary since any kind of love story—no matter how vague—only made me more miserable. I had even gone so far as to have the realization that I was holding onto the pain because it still provided a connection or attachment to this guy. And yet, knowing this and so much more, failed to lift me out of it all.

And there on the tube, they were showing this primitive method of catching live monkeys. What they were doing was putting an orange into a small jug or jar and attaching it to the ground or a tree (people do this not the monkeys). There was a small opening in the jar, just big enough for the monkey to get his or her hand through. When the monkey would see this orange, it feels like it can't do without, it reaches through the hole and grabs it. But the opening is too small for the monkey to get its hand out *as long as it is holding the orange*. *Violà*. Trapped live undamaged monkey.

These monkeys would stay there for days, even starve, until the people would come by to scoop them up. I was watching this thinking deep spiritual thoughts along the lines of: "stupid monkeys," when I finally receive the first message from spirit or "the guys" in months. You've probably gathered that they hinted...strongly, that these monkeys and I had more in common than an ancestor.

I share this tale not simply because of a desire to humiliate myself in public. I far prefer to do so one-on-one or in small groups. If it has any resonance for you, I hope that you will recall its gentle message in times of internal strife. "Drop the orange, and nobody gets hurt!"

As I said initially of progress, growth is less of an arc and more of a coil wrapping around itself, rising each time it goes around. That's life on a larger scale, I believe. I don't really believe in reincarnation anymore as only one soul coming back repeatedly. I believe each soul is given but one lifetime. What gives the illusion of past lives is that we are part of an oversoul, which, like fingers attached to a hand, may have ten or twelve souls that, though separate and distinct, tap into an oversoul that forms something of a hub that joins them.

I believe what gives the illusion of reincarnation is the oversoul lending a soul incarnate information and experiential substance from other souls joined to it. We have a direct connection to those other souls, which may act as past lives since all twelve are not incarnate at one time. Whether a given oversoul is made up of six sets of twin flames is unknown to me but it would make sense if it was. What is clear is that there is some substantial exchange among the given souls. All this lends the appearance of reincarnation. I suppose what I am saying can be a form of reincarnation just explained a little differently than simply dying and coming back as another person. I believe you die and another soul born has direct connection to the information of your soul and lifetime but is not necessarily specifically *you*. And I believe that the lessons we learn here may indeed be shared with the others in our cadre. It's rather like a television in which the same pixels are used to form one picture and later a totally different image still accessing the same pixels just reconfigured/re-colored, or recycled to form the new image.

What is more at issue is that at some point in the hierarchy of soul to oversoul and on up, we are all part of one Christ mind that is a direct aspect of God the All. And that He is eager for our return even though, since linear time only exists in the lower realms such as the physical and some alternate version of time in the etheric and astral realms, at a certain point there is no time, and so if we ever were One, we already are again.

The ultimate Truth is we never left. In the end of *The Wizard of Oz*, which, like *Star Wars*, is the perfect hero's journey movie. Dorothy wakes up to find she is home again—and actually never left to begin with—although she is changed by her journey through Oz, despite it not having been ultimately real. I believe we shall experience something of that in the end. But it will be like gold going through the refiner's fire where it relinquishes its bonds, blows apart at a molecular level, drops its impurities, and comes back together again as the purified gold we cherish with all its adherent qualities. We will have been refined by our journey through this world of illusions and, with any luck, be better for it.

PAY NO ATTENTION TO THE MAN BEHIND THE CURTAIN

Love does not hide behind a veil, or cloak itself in mystery. Love begs union. Love longs to be known. Love yearns to be seen in truth. God longs to know himself through us;

see himself in us. The most ardent and best intentioned of us will often find within, a knee-jerk response to avoid asking the tough questions of God; fearful that we will discover that this thing our hearts demand we acknowledge, will reveal itself to be nothing more than myth—fluff and faerie dust.

True faith is found in the act of hunkering down and entering that sacred place we both need and fear, entrusting that this leap will end in the secure knowing of our union with the divine—that we will wind up in the unfailing arms of Love rather than as one more unidentifiable splotch of roadkill on the highway of existence. But that leap requires trust and faith. I ventured forth and I leapt, and I can honestly say God caught me. It was only later when fear got a hold of me further down the line, that things went awry.

God begs entreaty. Love can stand up to challenge. That is not the question. The question is, can we? That's the true core fear at work in the equation, for we do understand on some level that these things we profess to believe which I have sketched out here as true operating principles, and the mundane existence we experience, are mutually exclusive. Something's got to give. The trouble is that we have culturally rejected the metaphysical Truth, dismissing and demeaning it; and have embraced the lie as real, rationalizing it as being realistic, prudent. We've gathered it to our bosom and try not to fear, though we feel the tip of the thinly covered point of its blade pressing into our flesh, leaving us trying not to flinch as it pierces our skin.

It behooves us to embrace the Reality that is the greater Truth—that God, and therefore Love, is the way to go. It is the proper place to invest our faith. We all have faith, it is simply a matter of what we place it in. Most of us have been trained to only lend our faith to that which is quantifiable; directly experiential through our five senses. That slight shift in where we place our true faith is the basis of that difference. It is not so hard really, but we generally have been taught great resistance to it. Why? Because we have had fear thrust upon us at every turn. We are willing to pour our faith into anything but each other. Even God is viable until we mention that there is no place where God ends and others begin. That faith in God is inherently faith in one another—in the goodness in others' hearts, for all that can possibly bring us joy and peace requires some level of trust in one another. Everything that could bring us happiness is a cooperative effort. Our happiness and fulfillment of our dreams truly does depend at least to some extent on cooperation and support—the love of another for its accomplishment.

No man is an island, and until we grow to trust one another with our hearts, we are doomed to a less than joyful existence. There is no such thing as having your own little things with God off in a corner somewhere away from all others. That sounds like the safe way to go, but God does not work like that. God has instituted at a core level that one man's happiness depends on the goodness of another. It's simply hard-wired that way. But once that is established know, too, then that others' happiness depends in part on your cooperation or good intentions as well, and the more you can lend yourself to that effort, the happier you will be. For the universe works in such a way that once we engage in a loving fashion that helps others to manifest their dreams and goals, we will, in turn, feel more deserving of others helping us to achieve ours as well. And that's where you want to get to. God cannot do for us, what He cannot do through us. Therefore, the more we lend ourselves to God's will fulfilled, the greater our chances are of achieving not just the momentary distraction from our own pain, which generally is enough to pass for happiness in our society; but true joy and happiness that need not end. You only get to take with you that which you can carry in your heart and soul. Fill that vessel as fully as you can and you will be rich indeed.

FATHER KNOWS BEST

I mentioned that we are hardwired to lean on God, so let's take a moment to discuss the option of doing things "by ourselves," we tireless members of the "He-Man Deity Haters Club—No Gods Allowed. This Means U." I mentioned that God's will is in service of what will *genuinely* make us happy, although we are certainly free to disagree. (We'll be wrong, but we can do it.) We are, in many cases, able to manifest our own version of what will make us happy. Not always, but quite often we know better, but for some reason we disregard this instinct and plow ahead anyway. This endeavor will actually carry us farther from the real mark (though its collapse may also drop us at God's feet). Although it is possible for it to be achieved, If it is not in our best interest, the universe will not contribute to our cause regardless of how much we whine, bargain, or pretty it up

As they say, you can put an evening gown on a sow, but all you have is a pig in a dress. Most of us first come to this work with a bevy of our own hard-won porcine prom queens in tow and yet remain unfulfilled. Actually, the fact that we have succeeded in manifesting our will time and time again and are still not really happy, is proof that we really don't know best in this matter. The difference between "our way" and the far more desirable "high way" is outside help. To use a sailing analogy, it's the difference between sailing into shore with the wind at our back versus having to tack.

Just so there is no misunderstanding, please know that spirituality will not help us attain safety through impenetrability or joy through material accumulation. I'm sure if these actually addressed our real needs, it would; however, one of the things we learn as we move through this work, is that quite often what is in need of change is not God's response, but our request. Not that there's anything wrong with abundance, financial or otherwise. I know it is said that love of money is the root of all evil, but I would clarify that money itself does not warp people. It is not so much that it modifies someone as it amplifies them, and what generally is amplified is an imbalanced value system. You make a useful product and someone buys it, it is a win-win for you both. That is righteous exchange.

When money becomes an issue, it is generally because it is of an ilk where it is financial gain at someone else's expense. In this idea we bought into the notion that it is simply part of business as usual, which is utter nonsense. I stress again that the biggest problem we face in this world today is that we value short-term economic gain over humanity, and until we reverse this value system, we are on an ocean liner headed for an iceberg. And the hour is late. Our current system is literally unsustainable so the time is now and it starts with you and I, holding ourselves and others accountable. This is so vitally important. We need to stop merely asking if something is legal and start asking, but is it right? Is it righteous? Is it good?

Acceptance of God is really self-acceptance, because God is not out there somewhere separate and apart from, He is the very best in each and every one of us. You learn to trust yourself with yourself, creating a space where you feel you are safe with yourself—that you are not going to thrust yourself into situations that are dangerous to you on any level. Nor are you going to try and sabotage what you're attempting to create. So how do we get there?

Firstly, remember that it is not the self that you've created as a personality that you are learning to accept and love, it is the Self that God created deep within you that you are learning to discover and subsequently love and trust. That authentic Self, which some call the Christ mind, the Shakina, or the Buddha mind, was created perfectly for it is of God. It is our spirit. It's the spark of the divine within each and every one of us. That is what we hope to align with, as best we can muster on the earth plane, with all our human frailties. But those frailties transform into our strengths as we move through our spiritual practice. It is spiritual alchemy where you shift an energy quality from its fear-based attribute to the positive attribute of the same quality in service of love. You don't have to try to make it happen for that is like seeking happiness.

Happiness as a direct goal never works out, or it is fleeting. To last, happiness must be a byproduct of the goal of loving the very best we can; seeing the innocence in our brother instead of his guilt. It is the Self that God endowed us with that His will urges us to be. It is itself one of love, which has a conduit to the divine, meaning it is ultimately trustworthy. That is The Self with the capital S. The self that is a small s self, is largely comprised as a walking defense mechanism, for it is born of the ego. It is not our true Self and to put stock in it does not serve us.

As I said earlier, spiritual development is not really a self-help paradigm. This is why. The self as we refer to it, is not the solution but the problem in that it constantly tries to substitute the ego's self for the Authentic Self. It is that part of our being centered in the mind that the ego whispers its will into urging us to enact it and its fear base in the world.

Remember that the ego does not reveal itself as ego, otherwise we wouldn't listen to it. It generally comes to us urging us to be prudent, or in defense of self, or self-righteous. It poses as self-care. It's the part of us that says that that person is not treating us right, and don't they know who I am, and if someone gets something there will be less for me, for I can't trust love of my heart, because it's hurt me in the past. But again, I say that Love will never lead you into harm; that there is always a detour into fear before the situation sours.

It's not love that cannot be trusted, its fear that cannot be trusted. Despite what the ego-based world would say. It is only when we're defenseless that we are safe. Our hearts will never lie, given that they have that conduit to God, who has the view both above and through the playing field, and can therefore calculate all sorts of elements of which our minds are unaware.

We can discern the voice of the ego versus the still small voice of God, for they have a completely different tone. One is infused with love and the other is infused with fear. Most of us don't really have a problem discerning one from the other so much as we have a problem choosing love over fear. When fear tells us that we have every reason to protect ourselves, and that this or that would be the clever thing to do right at a given moment, we do it without thinking it through. We are impulsive. That's one of the things ego uses in its vast arsenal, is it makes us fearful, so we act on impulse instead of decision. Reaction instead of choice.

But God is willing to earn our trust and allow love to lead us out of this dream that has become a nightmare. If we are having trouble discerning love from fear, it is because we are in the grip of fear. Its clouds block the sun and the ego will try and convince us that the sun has been extinguished. This is no truer of love and God, than it is of the sun. The best way to break this hold is to connect with someone else with loving intent. Merely focus on another person with love and the fear will fall away. To focus on another person with love takes you out of yourself, and all that self-consciousness drops, and you suddenly are not merely comfortable, but captivating. When in doubt, make a few phone calls, and ask someone how their day is going; wish them a good day, try to do so without talking about yourself or at least keeping it to a minimum. Reach out. Fear is inevitably about contracting and retracting. It wants us to withdraw from trusting people and instead turn to things, and to counter this with an extension of love however small, restores our equanimity.

The more you choose love, the more you draw forth your authentic Self into being as a physical incarnation and the more you do this, the more you develop and grow that conduit, that relationship with God, the easier and easier it is to feel when we are out of alignment. People will begin to say that we are changing for the better; that we seem so different now. But ironically, this is not how we will experience it inside, for inside it will seem to us that we are merely becoming more and more our real Self. In short, because we actually are doing just that.

I remember in my younger days, people would always say to me, just be yourself and I would always think silently, "I wouldn't know where to begin; or, you've got to come up with a better plan than that, Jeff." Now I understand what they were talking about. I was simply considering the wrong part of myself.

The only time I got advice to the contrary—and it was bad advice, very bad advice indeed—was back many years ago when I was first becoming friends with Angelina Jolie. She was delightful. Warm and loving, and bright and everything you would hope she would be. And I liked her very much, but then I became aware of her work and who she was and she was just emerging as a star. And I did something incredibly stupid. I listened to a friend of mine who said that there was no way she would want to really befriend me further unless I learned how to be cool. To just act like I didn't care about things and well, "Cool." I was feeling insecure and also my father had just died and I was trying desperately to raise money to keep my step-mother from losing the house, so I was a little unhinged to begin with, but I stupidly took his advice and adopted my idea of cool which translated into uncaring "too cool for school" persona and I hated cool so naturally I adopted the very worst qualities of that persona. Well, we were talking one day and she said she would like to work with me and get me a part in an upcoming film that she was considering making. I was very excited and thankful but instead of being genuine and myself I decided then and there to do a 180 and take this guy's advice and play it cool because I was feeling nervous and anything but cool.

Well, God save me from cool. I actually said something like yeah, let someone else pay for us to hang out or something equally disastrous. Well, it was not in character for me and it went over with a thud. And soon after the friendship cooled dramatically. And ended. It was a big blood lesson there. I will never again try to play it cool. Playing it cool is nothing more than an investment in pure unmitigated ego. In this case, it came across as my being the biggest jerk in the world. I regret it greatly not because of the loss of opportunity professionally, but because I believe I hurt her feelings and she had been nothing but warm and generous and wonderful with me. I honestly liked her very much as a person. I was utterly careless in the relationship and I will never do that again. So, from that disaster I have learned the only thing that works for me is to do my best to be as loving as I can be and allow that Self, my best Self to come forth and cultivate the best in myself, and allow for vulnerability; and leave cool for the hipsters and posers.

HOLDING THE VOID

Regarding vulnerability, it is a Yin quality, and we tend to have a diminished appreciation for those things associated with the Yin aspect of, well, everything. But there is great power in the Yin aspect of creation. As in nature, it is less showy than the Yang counterpart, but it is equal in its power and necessity. There is no Yang independent of Yin, and vice versa. But because we live in a patriarchy (probably a societal hangover from the Christian predominance in our culture, which is definitely patriarchal), whatever the source, the problem exists in that we devalue the Yin or feminine nature in our society, and that needs to be addressed. It's part of wanting the front of something without the attached back end coming with it. The Yin has great power because it receives the Yang and its form dictates the Yang's response.

For instance, there is a great power in what I call "holding the void." This is a Yin or feminine power, though it can easily be adopted by both men and women. Nature abhors a vacuum, and people don't cotton to it much either. It bothers them. But that bother can be brought into service if you know how to manage it.

I saw a documentary once, and in it, in a seemingly inconsequential scene, a man and woman were in the kitchen talking as they went about preparing dinner; and I took notice when the woman asked a delicate question of the man and he seemed hesitant to answer. I could see it scan across her face that maybe she should jump in and rescue them from the awkward silence by couching the question differently, maybe less pointedly, more indirectly, or jumping in with an excuse that would let him off the hook. Then I saw resolve take the place of that momentary insecurity, and she gathered the courage to simply hold the void and wait for her husband to fill it. The discomfort in him grew but she held firm, didn't rescue him, and suddenly the husband kind of relinquished or caved a little, and answered the question squarely. I watched her smile with loving satisfaction, and I knew I had witnessed something interesting.

There is a power in holding the void, not just in that instance, but in a more general way. When we hold the void spiritually, the universe rushes to fill it with its complement in order that the void be aptly filled. But it is particularly important to hold the void in its natural state and to hold it fully not partially, meaning when we have a desire, and I mean a deep heartfelt desire, a void is formed and it has the distinct shape of that particular desire. As it arises, its complement is called forth on a psychic or spiritual level. Now what most of us do is we feel the void, and it is uncomfortable to feel a void. Instead of letting the call go out and draw in the proper respondent, we stuff the void with food or sex, or drugs and alcohol, shopping, etc. or even with our emotions. We look to mitigate it so it is not so uncomfortable to live with.

We hold the original desire in our heart but stuff the actual void in some way to ease our pain. What we don't realize is that a partial filling alters the shape of the void, and so although it continues to call to a complement that will fill it, the shape of the call is now warped and diminished so it doesn't call as strongly or specifically, and that's a problem. We've lessened our chances of calling forth a response that will meet our heart's desire. Addiction is so often about "feeding the hole," as my friend Martha used to say. Well, the truth is there is no hole to feed. Why? Because we are whole and good as God created us, and there is no place where God is not. But we do have desires that God Himself will strive to fulfill.

It's like filling a wine glass partially with liquid, and rubbing the rim to produce a musical tone. If you put something else in the glass it either changes the pitch, muffles the tone, or in the extreme, blots out the capacity to make sound with it at all, depending on what you used to stuff that void.

That is what happens on a spiritual level when we rush to fill the void the heart and soul is holding. While it is uncomfortable, I highly recommend holding the void in the same capacity as it has when it arises. The chances are far greater we will receive an appropriately satisfying answer to our call. And while this goes without saying, I'll say it anyway: God wants you to have your heart's desire met, because He loves you dearly. But God is also always looking for a win-win situation, and please know that your true heart's desire will never be at someone else's expense. If your deepest desire necessitates this, then you need to explore what ego may have seeped into it.

Bless in others what you would have for yourself. Celebrate their wins and you will feel much, much better about your chances of your own desires being met. Love well. Love often. And do the legwork. If your heart's desire is a relationship, you must hold the void, but do look for potential partners. Put yourself out there. We don't dismiss the Yang element; the doing element. Instead, we work the Yin and the Yang equally for they both have great power and are inseparable.

Marianne Williamson speaks about the need to develop our attitudinal musculature. And that's all spiritual development is. But you don't get there without practice. I'd like to share a prayer or affirmation that was given to me by my acupuncturist Susan Davis, who really did save my life and who irrevocably changed my outlook in the process for the better, reigniting me on the spiritual path. It goes:

I am entirely good and whole.
My heart is tender and strong.
I am surrounded by love.
I breathe it in to the depths of my being,
and breathe out that which binds me,
transformed and returned as my blessings.
I am one with the light.

I have found that affirmation helps me greatly when I am feeling off-center or simply want to thank God for my life. I believe that a lot of our real problem is that we've fallen asleep to who we are and who our Father is. All manner of problems arise from this confusion, and the above helps me to remember myself when I am in doubt or despair and confusion.

The rest is all lateral, meaning your particular ego wounding is no more or less pretty than mine. It's merely presenting differently, so it's simply unfair to compare and contrast. You may have it together in one area that I don't, and vice versa. But here's where union really counts in that God may send you to me for a friendship, and part of that friendship may be my learning from you how to succeed in that area in question from watching your excellence in it, and the same may be true for you with some area in which I have expertise and you're seeking improvement. All this is part of loving well, but this is all part of how we grow through each other and why union is so important.

ANOTHER VICTIM OF THE MISTLETOE WARS

This heading was a message given to me by Spirit in the midst of my failing in the relationship with my twin flame. It was their humorous way of warning me not to become a victim in love. I was warned in advance that despite destiny, a destined relationship can still be blown if not handled with the care and reverence it deserves. Loving relationships are a beautiful thing, to be honored and cherished. And not every relationship has romantic and sexual form as its pinnacle. Sometimes true friendship is the pinnacle of the relationship. At some point, the messages you receive will instruct you in drawing to you your Truly Beloved. Not your soul mate but your twin flame, which is your spiritual counterpart; your perfect complement, who has the capacity to love you like no one else. So, when you are courted by Him or Her, roll with it and surrender to the immense love being offered you. This is not to say things may not be occasionally rocky because, though you will feel intensely drawn to them, they also will bring up your deepest wounding to be healed and that can be very messy or off-putting.

Boundaries that are effective and genuine, are also fluid, strong, and clear. Once you are in touch with the Holy Spirit within you, setting boundaries comes naturally as an extension of love. You get very content and happy, loving and being loved in the world, so that when someone or something comes along that is out of sync with that energy pattern, we notice it. Often before it even fully arrives. That clarity is a gift of spiritual development. Clear Sight. And you trust your heart to guide you as to when and how to set a boundary with someone.

We have a much better chance of working through an issue if we don't make the other person the issue. Instead, you call out the behavior itself, then how it makes you feel, and finally, what God has told you should be done about it. And you don't actually say this is what God told me. That's very off-putting to others because it sounds arrogant and uncontestable.

You can have a situation where you need to draw a line on some form of behavior that is just unacceptable. Yet in another situation that seems similar in form, you may receive a different suggestion entirely and both will be appropriate to their specific dynamic. That's how we set boundaries. And we allow them to change as trust grows. Rigid boundaries that function as strict walls fail us in the end because we usually, in applying a one-size-fits-all form of boundary setting, exclude someone or something that would have been so right for our growth, and we've cut it off by applying the same wall for each similar situation. We miss out on so much that way. Sometimes the loving response is no. There's no arguing that, but how you frame it so that it may be accepted by the other person is of utmost importance.

I used to have an issue around boundaries. The problem was that I didn't really have any, which got me into trouble as people would take advantage of me and I never knew when to call a halt to it. I was loyal, but to a fault. Then one day I realized that the problem was not really boundaries but integrity. Mind, body, spirit, all moving as one—serving one goal. An example of this is in *Wizard of Oz* when Dorothy melts the witch with water, which symbolically is spirit casting out ego. It was a reflexive act of love to save the scarecrow when she unthinkingly grabbed the bucket and threw the water on him; her mind, body, and spirit were all reflexively serving love, and in that moment, she was galvanized with integrity and that's what kills the ego. That initial act of integrity or galvanizing will happen reflexively at some point initially – that will draw our focus to it, but then we must work at it for continued success to occur.

Part of that success is in how we set boundaries. We learn what feels in and out of integrity because to have a hard and fast rule about anything weighs us down and impedes us. We miss opportunities and block things that could serve us or let in things that harm us in the end. It has to be situation by situation. And that's what integrity is about.

Integrity emanates from the spirit and the heart, and then the consciousness, and the body follow. We have to keep checking into our hearts when we make decisions, and when we sense something is not of love that's been presented to us, we will notice that if we stay in integrity, we will know how to proceed. We will indeed know when to call a halt to things and when we need to hang in there and work through the issues at hand.

One thing I have noticed is that when a friend is asked regarding an argument or whatever happens to have come up that is unpleasant between two lovers, the advice will invariably be to dump that guy or girl. I attribute this to just dismissiveness. I would not be so quick to follow that advice because issues are going to come up and it's important to stay present with someone even if you have to take some time apart to think. If you drop everyone who disappoints you, you're going to end up very alone, because eventually everyone will disappoint you to some degree. But also, it's not appropriate to put all your needs and wants on one person. This is a lesson it would've served me to learn much sooner than I did.

Be considerate and allow the person to save face if at all possible. Setting a boundary does not have to be an attack energy. If it is rooted in love, and that includes self-love, and the need to protect our base that we may remain fully functional in the world, then so be it. It will ring true, and if it speaks to the heart instead of the defenses of the mind, then you will have done a great job. But like anything else, it requires actual practice to be able to do it with some grace and ease.

It comes down to owning your "yes" and owning your "no" again. Both can spring from love and should. If you set a boundary with someone and there's an attack in it, then we're back at square one with the sword falling on our head not theirs. Though they probably will be tempted to attack back, even if they don't, you will feel like they have, and you'll be in the thrall of ego until you can find your release to go home and re-center again, which you do by asking forgiveness and repair of the Holy Spirit who is always willing to help you mend your mistakes.

Remember that you are not your mistakes any more than you are your achievements. One of the blood lessons I learned as an actor was to remember "I am not my work." My work comes from me but it's not my identity. Most of us have a very narrow sense of identity, consisting of far too many labels; and these labels we place on ourselves defining us are not expansive enough to really fulfill their role.

And, we are not our feelings. We *have* our feelings, but they don't define us. Knowing that frees you up from being in compulsion or reaction. It brings you back to choice and responsiveness. We are more than our thoughts, too. We are children of God, and as such we have creative power that cannot be extinguished. That's not up to us to choose. What is up for choice is what we will create.

It's as if we have a giant laser that is always on. The question is, do we cure someone's sight or sear off the top of the couch with it. When you're in love and supported dearly by another, you garner more courage, and courage is needed to choose love in the face of some of the things we encounter in the world today. Try not to let the fears of the world press you into making a false or hasty choice. We've wasted too much time as a civilization choosing fear and we're no safer than we were before. In fact, things are more unsafe and insane than ever before in history.

We've been so scared of trusting love, despite our claims that it is the greatest power in the universe. We say that, but it's time we act on commitment to that belief. After all, we've tried everything else. The answer to every problem or call to love, is a face of love. A deeply loving relationship allows you a safe haven where you can feel loved in a way that you can take in the music of it. You can breathe it in and let it nurture you. It also acts as a defining element then, so when something adverse to love comes along it jars us. It bothers us. And well it should. But don't feed on the fear. Let that go. Acknowledge the problem or risk; pray; and choose love anyway. For love is disarming, and something shifts in people when your words and presence strike that ring of truth. It calls their heart to open as well. And when you're engaged with someone who also is coming from a loving choice, you are joined by God. Nothing less than that. And God really does exist in a palpable way.

When you choose love, all the universe moves with you; and eventually you begin to see evidence of that. Little shards of proof in the way of synchronicities or results that were on-the-money despite a lack of knowledge of some of the obstacles. That's God's hand showing. And that's encouraging for the next choice that arises. And don't believe in anything that claims you have no choice. You do. Always. It is part of our creation that cannot be altered. So, if your feelings force you into a thought pattern of escape or attack and the accompanying feeling you have to do it, that you have no choice in the matter, remember who you are and who made you, and the door will open and you will see room for choice again.

HOME TO STAY

Earlier I mentioned that growth is hardly an ever-upward arc, but is cyclical, in that you end up in the same place with similar circumstances occurring but due to accomplishing the hero's journey, you arrive home again with a new awareness, and it is that new awareness that changes everything. So it is with the homecoming. The archetypal hero journey concludes with the return home. Home to stay. While this is true metaphorically, the journey doesn't truly end there. Home becomes synonymous with being centered and in the flow of life; well connected to our higher power, which is our source for inspiration and simple decision-making as well. The full gamut. Having stilled the ego, we are released, and like the cork held underwater, once released, we bob to the surface in keeping with our natural buoyancy. The journey doesn't end. It will never end until we are once again reunited with God the All. All of us. Until then, the journey continues, but something has shifted deeply when we find home again. We tend not to invest so much in chasing things. Our core values tend to deepen and be marked with greater humanity; and we let life come to us rather than pursuing things "out there." Our new sense of being allows us instead to draw things in to ourselves. Information, events, people, and opportunities for happiness tend to flow our way. And we take them in and allow them to nurture us and to grow from them.

Our learning is ongoing. It bears repeating, we love the very best we can all ways because frankly, we need the practice. Lastly, the effective mark of our transformation is a growing ease. Ease within and without. This is not to say that there will be a lack of drama as we grow and offer ourselves more bravely to the world, but that our lives will be marked by a higher drama, rather than the petty cheap drama that too often stains people's lives. No longer will we feel crippled by our own shortcomings. We will practice their transformation; their transmutation to be more specific, as we continue to practice spiritual alchemy—the art of allowing a quality formerly held in the clutches of fear to be moved along the spectrum to its being in service of love.

We no longer underestimate love and the power it has to transform. This is not to say we will be home free—without pain or challenges—but we will regard them a bit differently. We will see how in serving God and others that these challenges offer an opportunity along with their grit for us to become more and more our best selves. Our higher Self, for God is within us and so to serve God is in fact to serve our highest good; and since God desires a win-win situation, we also invariably serve the world as we strive to live more authentically. We tend to view our egos more objectively, no longer seeking to keep them hidden from ourselves but instead to reveal their machinations that we may avoid playing into their hands. When we begin to observe our ego states, we will invariably find we have a growing spiritual and emotional intelligence that informs the work of living an honorable life. Our intuition grows increasingly as we nurture and cultivate it. And we find things are more readily apparent to us, for we are less likely to participate in the games of joining in the mystery of things when there's a problem.

This striving to see things as they are in order that we may bring about change lends us a clarity that will simply become innate and natural. But there is always something new to learn, and we are not designed to rest on our laurels. I believe that our only choice is whether we learn through joy or pain, and my experience is that if you continue to strive to learn even when things are going well, it will keep you in good stead. Some painful lessons can be avoided if you are learning them before it reaches that point; despite that, most of us end up learning through pain; though it is actually our default position to learn through joy, meaning that is God's desired choice for us. If we strive to stay more present and available on a daily basis the way becomes clearer and the road broader. We cast our net further and wider and do our best to love any and all who are brought into our care every day. And it will begin to feel like everyone you interact with has the potential to be a holy encounter. And so we strive to make it so.

Life is an ongoing journey, but returning home to yourself and God time after time, gets easier. Some of the markers or "crumbs" become more established, and some of the tools better honed, and with these you will find it is the journey itself that is the most important. The journey is the destination—the means is the ends. And may I be the first to say, "Welcome Home."

Angels, Devils, Spiritual Rebels
Wayne Saalman

[NOTE: This is the chapter 27 from Wayne Saalman's book The Dream Illuminati: A Global Revolution Takes Flight *(New Falcon Publications). The book aims to challenge readers to investigate their belief systems in order to re-evaluate, and ultimately expand, their world view.]*

On the third day after the massacres in New York and San Francisco, and the bombings in Chicago and Atlanta, it was time to bury the dead.

In New York, there was grieving of a magnitude not seen for years. For thirteen Vimanians had literally fallen from the sky and the funeral was massive, so huge in fact, that a four block radius had to be cordoned off and closed to all traffic in that vicinity.

As a mark of solidarity, the cathedrals in Chicago and Atlanta also held ceremonies within their naves at the same time, and this despite the gaping holes in the sides of their buildings.

In San Francisco, the lone police officer who had been slain was buried in a private ceremony, while in Vimana Cathedral, there were six to be eulogized. The ceremony, now in progress, was also of a magnitude that had not been seen in the city in years. It was full of weeping and joy, as love and condolences went out to the families... And each and all who spoke decried the senselessness of the killings.

Outside the cathedral in the four cities, thousands lined the streets, inevitably some for and some against the Order, but most of the voices were muted now out of respect for the dead and only the national and international media coverage proved to be maddening for everyone involved.

Indeed, story after story was being told, and eulogy after eulogy delivered. The surprise guest in San Francisco was the Reverend Donovan Reaves who strolled humbly into the great nave beside his niece, Heather, and he was pushing Shane Ridley in a chair. His own comment to the clamoring media: "God Almighty has commanded, "Thou shalt not kill." Yet, some of our own have done just that and it is never right. I am here in San Francisco, therefore, out of respect for the dead and to honor the Word of God. Let us heed that Word. Let us all resolve to live together in peace for the sake of the world. Amen."

As the eyes of the world looked on, Kelby rose at last to speak, to deliver the final homily, and to put the tragedy to rest. But Kelby knew that this words would have a limited impact. Those who did not want to hear, would not hear, though his voice would be amplified and carried live across the entire planet. On this day there would be no missing his voice. But not everyone with ears to hear would hear it.

Nevertheless, certain issues needed to be addressed and Kelby intended to do just that.

"Ladies and gentlemen, I speak to you today from the heart," he began, "sad for the loss of life, but hopeful too that greater understanding will prevent further bloodshed in the future and that this tragic occasion will serve to awaken all of us to the preciousness of life and the sanctity of it. There is no point in my setting up an 'us' and 'them' scenario here and arguing that 'we' are better or more right than 'them' and calling for vengeance against the perpetrators of these crimes. Of course certain individuals have conspired to harm us and *have* harmed us. They have done *far more* than simply harm us, they have murdered our own. But should we condemn the individuals alone or the groups to which they belong? Tyler Evans was a Christian and the three gunmen in New York were allegedly, 'Agents of Babylon'. Is traditional Christianity the enemy then? And the agents of Babylon? And are these 'agents', as some say, the Illuminati in disguise? Are they part of a secret Brotherhood? Could they be an extremist faction of the Freemasons as some insist? Or is it the Vatican that colludes with the Brotherhood? Or the Freemason *and* the Catholic Church? In other words, both Protestants and Catholics?! Who are the enemies of the Order of Vimana?

"Some, many, have been editorializing in the last twenty four hours that the Brotherhood is actually *pro*-Vimana and that they perpetrated the whole sniper incident in New York in an effort to gain public sympathy for Vimana. They did this, according to this line of reasoning, so that the dominant social trend in America, and indeed the whole planet, will now move another step closer to a New World Order and that New World Order will effectively supplant traditional Christianity and consolidate power even more-so for the secular government. For this religion they say has proven to be one that has generated conflict. So to have Judaism and the Islamic faith. The proof of that is not just in the Middle East, but all over the planet these days. But nationalism too has caused conflict. Not merely regional conflicts, but world wars. Nevertheless, many of these same writers and pundits on television have noted that such conflicts have actually *served* the world economy and the Powers That Be up to now. It has funneled wealth beyond belief into the hands of these powers.

"Of course, these are different times and different times can call for a change of strategy, a fresh approach. Some say there *should be* a World Government at last. For the world is now very much operating with a global economy. And perhaps it is time for humanity to see the end of entrenched nationalism and religious sectarianism, because our oil resources, which have driven the engine of the global economy for so long now, are dwindling. The planet is polluted now certainly because of our overuse of fossil fuels and the very survival of the earth is at stake finally. The Vimana is obviously the vehicle of the future, they argue. It doesn't pollute and it uses very little fuel of a type which is quite abundant. And once it is licensed for general use by the public, which should be quite soon, these flying machines will be sold to the public and the production of these units will generate jobs, an there will be *serious funds* generated for the world markets and that will greatly enhance the global economy.

"It's a new day, these voices say, and the Powers That Be know that and they are acting on it. They want to move the world in a certain direction and, to do that, certain things must happen and happen fast. We are indeed in a world crisis. No one can doubt that. The fact of it is all around us.

"Many, of course, will say that such talk is nonsense. That the Babylon thing is a cover story for Christian or Islamic terrorists and so on. They will say that it's a menacing and complex world that we live in now and only time and patient investigations by the FBI, by state and local police, will solve this mysterious crime. But how do we answer it all today? How do we make *sense* of it all as we gather here together at this very moment?

"I don't pretend to have all of the answers. But I do have my own insights and I feel that I must speak out today as best I can. I think that we are living in a time of great change and great revelation. A time of great awakening. And though many of the sages in the past have known it and have been telling us this for centuries and millenniums, those who are awakening now are finally fully realizing something very important: that we live in a world of duality, that everything in this world, in fact, is *predicated* on duality and that duality is at the very root of all of our problems.

"What is duality? It is matter and spirit, it is light and dark, protons and electrons, positive and negative energies, subject and object, self and other, you and me... It is good and evil too. From the very inception of life as we know it, dualism is inherent. There is no ignoring it or escaping it. Once this universe was created, absolutely everything within it was subject to dualism. On this science and religion totally agree.

"The point is: there are indeed positive forces in this world and negative forces. They are within each of us and in everyone on the planet. They are in everything that lives on the earth. And we might call these positive and negative forces, Christly forces and Luciferian forces. The Hindus would say they are emanations of Vishnu, the creator, and Shiva, the destroyer. Buddhists would see these forces as impersonal *karmic* forces. They would say that there are no *beings,* or no God, generating these forces, but simply life itself creating them or the universe itself creating them. They would say that we ourselves *are* those forces, and that what we *think, say and do* quite simply comes back to us.

"But labels are just that: labels. We mustn't be fooled by words. Words are a human creation. There is nothing *absolute* about language.

"Still, we *do* think of language as absolute and millions of people down through the centuries have, over and again, fought and killed each other over words and labels. But this is a grave error and always was. The Judeo-Christian-Islamic traditions have been some of the most combative traditions in the world because of words and labels, and especially because of the insistence by so many within these particular traditions that their Holy Books are the absolute, *literal* Word of Yahweh or Allah.

"But is that in fact true? Leaving Islam aside for the moment, let me just give a few examples from the Judeo-Christian Bible that indicates contradiction, the most obvious being God's commandment that 'Thou shall not kill' and then doing that over and over again, smiting entire cities in some cases. If this isn't contradictory, then what is? And if there *is* only one Son of God as Christians insist, then why does the first book of their Bible, Genesis, in Chapter 6 say, 'And it came to pass, when men began to multiply on the face of the earth, and daughters were born unto them, that the Sons of God saw the daughters of men and they were fair; and took them wives all of which they chose.' What does this statement mean if not what it claims to mean? And in the original Greek, the Bible speaks of God as the *Elohim* which is actually a plural form that refers not simply to a monotheistic Deity, but to the *gods*.

"When we examine the four gospels too, Matthew, Mark, Luke and John, we find that the stories there don't always tally.

For example, after the crucifixion, once Jesus had been laid to rest in the stone sepulcher, Saint Matthew says that an angel descended from heaven and rolled back the stone on the third day and sat upon it, that the risen Jesus had left the tomb. In Saint Mark the account states that a young man in a white garment was within the empty tomb when the first persons arrived to look in on the body. In Saint Luke, there are *two* men in shining garments and in Saint John *two angels* dressed all in white.

"So if the Bible is literally true, why do we have these discrepancies? And why do we have the prophet Isaiah talking about dragons in Chapter 13, Verse 22, and about fiery flying serpent in Chapter 30, Verse 6 if dragons and flying serpents are unreal? Isaiah speaks of dragons again in Chapter 34, Verse 13, as well as about satyrs in Verse 14 of that same chapter. If these creatures never existed, what is Isaiah talking about? And who are the *Nefilim* that are alluded to in Genesis? Most early translators simply called them giants. Chapter 6, Verse 6, states that, 'There were giants in the earth in those days; and also after that, when the Sons of God came in unto the daughters of men, and they bare children to them, the same became mighty men which were of old, men of renown.' So if there were indeed giants on the earth in those days, then where are the bones? Where is the proof? Or could these Nefilim be some other group? There is at least one highly regarded translator of ancient languages who says that this term really means, 'Those Who Descended' or 'Those Who Fell From the Heavens'. And if these beings are indeed the Sons of God and they did indeed interbreed with the daughters of men, we have a very interesting lineage springing up at this juncture in history. Some say that these very beings are the ones we now refer to as the Illuminati and that their symbol is the serpent, and also the dragon, and that they are with us still, and that they yet orchestrate events behind the scenes in this world of ours. Perhaps, then, they have even orchestrated these very events that have brought us here *today*...

"I will let you think on that... But I will point out one further facet to consider in this matter. The biblical story of the Garden of Eden says that God told Adam and Eve not to touch the fruit of a certain tree. And it states in Genesis, in Chapter 2, Verse 9, that, '...out of the ground made the Lord God to grow every tree that is pleasant to the sight, and good for food; the tree of life also in the midst of the garden, and the tree of knowledge of good and evil.' And then in Chapter 3, Verse 5, the 'Serpent' tells Eve that she should eat of the tree, 'For God doth know that in the day ye eat there-of, then your eyes shall be opened, and ye shall be as gods, knowing good and evil.' In the New Testament too, in John 10:34, Jesus cries out, echoing this idea, 'Is it not written in your law, I said, Ye are gods?"

"Can we really be as gods by eating of the tree of life and knowing good and evil? Can we be as gods if we but see into our essential nature, a nature predicated on dualism? Can we all be like the Gnostics of old, the first real Christians, whose very name means 'Knowers'? Can we too be like the initiates in the Pagan Mysteries who understood that knowledge of God was only possible if one had a direct spiritual epiphany or experience of God. Have you heard that in knowing yourself, you know God?"

"In the book of Isaiah in the Bible, Chapter 45, Verses 6 and 7, it states quite explicitly, 'I am the Lord and there is none else. I form the light, and create darkness: I make peace and create evil: I the Lord do all these things.'

"This is an amazing statement really. It is an *extraordinary admission*, in fact, and it is time that we all face the music together, that we face reality itself, and understand that by our very nature we are both peace loving at times and violent at times. We do good some days, but other days we can and do make terrible mistakes, and say things that we don't really mean, and we hurt our loved ones or our neighbor. Every human being acts impulsively at times, and quite selfishly too. We don't put others first sometimes and that is where we fall down. But if we truly understand what that means, that we are ever inherently dualistic beings, then we will certainly be more forgiving of ourselves and our fellow humans too. For everybody errs and loses their head sometimes. Mistakes are made.

"Originally, the word 'sin' was a term used in archery where a bows man misses the mark. That is sin exactly, I say. It is a missing of the mark, plain and simple. God surely understands that. It happens and it is forgivable because mortal beings err at times and do that. But if a person learns from a mistake, he or she grows.

Of course, if one *intends* to cause hurt or harm, that is evil. That is being a fool. For we do reap what we sow and such evil will certainly come back on us, and we will pay a great price. By *causing* others to suffer in this world, we cause *ourselves* to suffer.

"But we must show compassion to one and all, even the fools among us, because we are all alike in essence. And it doesn't really matter if we are natives of this earth or if we came here in ancient times from the heavens, from some other planet entirely. We are all members of God's family. Or to put it another way, we are all at one with what the Greeks called the *Pneuma*, the Spirit, and what the ancient Chinese called the *Tao*, the Hindus the *Akasha*, the Buddhists the *Buddha Mind*, and what scientists today call the Zero Point Field, that unnamable Original Essence or Force that gives rise to the quantum universe itself in all of its cosmic grandeur and diversity.

"But no matter how we look at these matters, nor what we decide about them, it is time for the ruling elite to begin treating every soul on this planet as equals finally and to begin showing us more mercy and to be more concerned with the plight of the poor, and with those who do not even have enough food or clean water for themselves. Conversely, it is also time for those who feel frustrated and powerless, and bitter towards those who rule and possess ungodly riches, to understand that such beings or people arrived at their position in life by sowing *positive* karmic seeds sometime in the past, seeds that blossomed in such a way that these beings now have what they have today. We all evolve at our own pace and in our own way. And in lifetime after lifetime, as souls reincarnate, they sometimes assume the role of the rich and sometimes the role of the poor. The Christian Gnostics believed this back in their day as much as the Hindus and the Buddhists do today. But once the concept of reincarnation was put into the hands of the ruling Roman emperors, Constantine and those after him, the concept was made a heresy. For it interfered with their own power. So they came up with an alternative concept. They told the people that they lived only *once* and that when they died they went either to heaven or hell for all of eternity. And only the priests could intermediate with God for them. And only the Church could save their souls from eternal damnation. But this concept is wrong. It is dead wrong. And it causes, and has caused, more suffering on this earth perhaps than any other concept ever devised.

"In truth, a soul lives on, over and over, projecting itself into various planes where certain causes and conditions prevail. But this life, or any other, is ultimately just another round on the Great Wheel of Life. And every lifetime is for learning spiritual lessons and for soul growth. And if we do happen to be one of the ruling elite in this lifetime, we would do well to remember those wise words from both Matthew and Mark in the Bible, 'For what shall it profit a man if he shall gain the whole world and lose his own soul?'

"I don't believe that Jesus exists the way that traditional Christianity says he exists, but I do believe that the *teachings of Jesus* are valid and true. I also believe that if anyone finds it spiritually uplifting and inspiring to believe in a personal Jesus, a Jesus who is the one and only Savior of Humankind, and if that article of faith gives hope and makes that person a better person, then fine. But don't be intolerant of those who see things otherwise.

I also don't believe that Satan exists the way that traditional religions in the West would have it. But there are *Luciferian* forces, forces that give rise to greed, to envy, selfishness, jealousy, hatred, vengeance and so on. These forces are indeed real, but they are quite simply lower forces that automatically arise in a dualistic world and serve to offer a contrast to the good. For without contrast, nothing can be understood nor have any meaning for us.

"And if you really find it difficult and hard to understand what the Order of Vimana is all about, I would say open up your Bible and look up some of the passages that I have quoted here today. Turn to Joel in the Old Testament and note where it says, 'Your sons and your daughters shall prophesy, and your old men shall dream dreams, your young men shall see visions.' Members of the Order do exactly that: dream dreams and then become visionaries. For that is precisely how the world evolves and becomes a better place, a place where people really *can* love their enemies, as Christ had hoped. A place where people are *pure in heart* and cease acting out of ulterior motives. Where the peacemakers really are blessed and called the children of God. Where people really do understand that we reap what we sow and that one should indeed love they neighbor as thyself.

" Please understand that if Jesus really did exist historically, then there is a certain fact about him that cannot be ignored. And it is this: Jesus was a rebel in his day! He set out to purposely overturn the old order and to break with many of the laws and customs of the Jewish culture. So maybe being spiritual rebel is not such a bad thing after all and maybe it is by rebellion that cultures break into new territory. The Protestant revolution is certainly another example of rebellion and the scale of that was enormous. So keep these points in mind when you go judging the actions of those of us involved with the Vimana movement. For we are not out to destroy the older order, but to enrich it and thereby create a fresh order, a twenty-first century order, but one founded on freedom and liberty for all, and not the dreaded 'New World Order' that is talked about by conspiracy theorists, an order that is as oppressive as ever, and as cold and calculating as ever, which many believe of the secret elite known as the Illuminati. What Vimanians want is a new order that rings as true in its metaphysics as in its science, an order that is compassionate and caring. We only ask that you give us a chance to prove that we can achieve that.

"To begin then, I will tell you that we Vimanians won't seek vengeance on those among you who have taken a certain twisted delight in the suffering that have been inflicted upon us. We know better. For we shall be as gods, knowing good and evil...We understand that karma isn't what happens to you, but *what you make happen*.

"And we know something else too... Christ is risen. The Redemption has come and the Ascension too. To fly, is to know that and to be at one with the angels.

"I stand before you grieving today, and emotionally exhausted but I am determined, more than ever, to help turn this world around and to put it on the right path. I am determined to do this regardless of what any religious extremists may throw at me or what any Powers That Be may do. And if the truth is to set us free, then we must *freely face the truth* and do what we know in our heart of hearts to be best.

There is a new heaven and a new earth before us now, and we must wipe away the tears from each other's eyes and see death for what it is, *transformation*. Death is not the opposite of life, but quite simply a process within it. The opposite of life is nothingness. But nothingness can never be. For life itself is the proof of that.

"All evolution within the *Whole* relies on the transformation of one thing into its opposite. So everything must return at last. Even me and even you. In some form. In some fresh form.

"With the deepest of perceptions, when one at last learns to identify with the eternal soul rather than with the mortal body, then one may finally understand that death is not the horror it is believed to be. Death is simply a part of the natural order in a world founded on causes and conditions. As the great poet,

Walt Whitman, once wrote in his poem *Song of Myself*,

> What do you think has become of the young and the old men (who have died)?
> And what do you think has become of the women and children?
> They are alive and well somewhere.
> The smallest sprout shows there is really no death...
> All goes onward and outward, nothing collapses,
> And to die is different from what any one supposed, and luckier.
> Has any one supposed it lucky to be born?
> I hasten to inform him or her it is just as lucky to die, and I know it.
> I pass death with the dying and birth with the new-washed babe, and am not contained between my hat and boots...
> I am not an earth or adjunct of the earth,
> I am the mate and companion of people, all just as immortal and fathomless as myself,
> (They do not know how immortal, but I know.)

"I know it too," Kelby said decisively. "And what is it, only suffering and death, that impels a human to even consider the spiritual side of life? It is death and suffering that causes us to have empathy and compassion, and to even *think about* anything beyond this material world.

"Maybe you do not know how immortal you are, but I know." He choked slightly on these words as they came forth from him now, but only because he was thinking of his own father, for he had read these very words of Whitman's a this father's funeral and they never failed to summon tremendous emotion.

But Kelby pressed on, paraphrasing the Bible now. "In that day, when such a perception fills us, there will be no more death, neither sorrow, nor crying, neither shall there be any more pain: for the former things are passed away, we will say. And joy and eternal bliss will be ours forever.

"Life is about one thing," he said, "spiritual enrichment. It is about spiritual enrichment and virtually all of our pleasures and pains contribute to that enrichment. So love life as it is and live it with exuberance an a pure heart. It is yours because you are lie. And I have had my say now and I can do little else only wish you peace forever and ever. Amen."

Contributing Authors

Chic Cicero has authored books on subjects including the Golden Dawn, tarot, and ceremonial magic with his wife, S. Tabatha Cicero. Having established a Golden Dawn temple in 1977, Chic was one of the key people who helped his friend Israel Regardie to resurrect a legitimate, initiatory branch of the Hermetic Order of the Golden Dawn in the United States in the early 1980s.

S. Tabatha Cicero is a member of several Co-Masonic, Martinist, and Rosicrucian organizations. She met her husband and co-author Chic Cicero in the early 1980s and the Golden Dawn system of magic has been her primary spiritual focus ever since.

Peter Conte carries forth the torch of the Magickal Childe Bookstore in New York City where he read Tarot cards for many years. Peter embodies the shop's motto, "Hard Core, New Age." He is currently writing a book on the Tarot which promises to be very thorough.

Lon Milo DuQuette is a noted Tantric authority who has written and taught extensively in the areas of Mysticism, Freemasonry, Tarot, Qabalah, ceremonial magic, Enochian magic, spirit evocation, and the Goetia. He is the coauthor with Christopher S. Hyatt of several New Falcon Publication titles.

Eric Gullichsen has been involved with computers and programming for more than four decades. He has written in the areas of hypertext, logic programming languages, and digital logic.

Steven Heller, Ph.D. was widely in demand as a clinician, lecturer and trainer of the Ericksonian method, which he helped develop, as well as his own method, Unconscious Restructuring. Dr. Heller received his Ph.D. in clinical psychology from California Western University, where his special area of study was hypnosis.

William S. Hyatt, the son of Christopher S. Hyatt, is a writer, an entrepreneur and a critical observer of human behavior in the style of his father.

Richard Kaczynski, Ph.D. is a psychologist specializing in non-mainstream religious beliefs. He has written extensively and lectured internationally on mystical and magical beliefs and practices.

Timothy Leary, Ph.D. was a respected Harvard psychology professor who became a guru for hundreds of thousands of people, espousing the use of the powerful hallucinogen LSD and other mind-altering drugs as a means of brain change. After he was forced out of academia, Leary became associated with many of the great names of the time including Aldous Huxley, Allen Ginsberg, William Burroughs and Charlie Mingus. He died in 1996. Dr. Leary is the author of the New Falcon titles: *What Does WoMan Want?*, *The Intelligence Agents*, *Info-Psychology*, and *Neuropolitique*.

Jeff Mandon has been a student of spiritual development for more than 45 years. Formerly an actor, Jeff has worked in theatre as well as both film and television. During the 1990s Jeff was one of the core cast of the show "In Our Lives," for which he wrote many episodes. His work garnered the Parents Choice Award, the Action for Children's Television award, and a regional Emmy nomination. The essay in this book is culled from his upcoming title, "*CRUMBS… And Other Things I've Followed Home*." Jeff has also worked as a sculptor primarily in the medium of cast bronze.

Osho, known also as Bhagwan Shree Rajneesh, was born in India in 1932 and died in 1990. He stands as one of the most famous religious leaders of modern times. He probably hold the record for being thrown out of, or refused entry into, the greatest number of countries in history. He is the author of the New Falcon title *Rebellion, Revolution & Religiousness*. His life and his work should be inspirations to rebels everywhere.

Dr. Israel Regardie was an Adept of the Golden Dawn. At an early age, Regardie worked as Aleister Crowley's personal secretary. Regardie was the messenger to the modern world charged with preserving the teachings of Crowley and the Golden Dawn. In addition to his extensive writings, Regardie practiced as a Chiropractor and Therapist. He taught psychiatry at the Los Angeles College of Chiropractic and contributed articles to many psychology magazines.

Wayne Saalman has traveled extensively throughout North America, Europe, Asia, Africa, and Australia in his quest for understanding and insight into the nature and historic origins of human metaphysics. A spiritual syncretist, he personally practices both Gnostic and Buddhist forms of meditation, and draws heavily on the shamanism, magick, yoga, Tantra, Tai Chi, and Chi Kung.

James Wasserman studied and practiced the magical system of Aleister Crowley since the late 1960s. He was a noted author of numerous books on esoteric symbolism, magick, and secret societies, as well as a passionate advocate for the values expressed in the Declaration of Independence, the U.S. Constitution, and the Bill of Rights. The photos he contributed to this book are shown in color in *Secrets of Masonic Washington*.

Dr. Jack S. Willis has graduate degrees in Biochemistry and Psychology and is a Doctor of Chiropractic Medicine. He trained in Reichian Therapy with Dr. Israel Regardie for nine years. A close friend of Dr. Hyatt's, he served as director of the Reichian Therapy Center in Los Angeles, California.

Robert Anton Wilson was the author of numerous books on such wide-ranging subjects as quantum mechanics, UFOs, history, science fiction, sex, mind-altering drugs, mysticism, scientists (pompous and otherwise), secret societies and, especially, human consciousness. They include the best selling New Falcon titles: *Cosmic Trigger Trilogy, Sex, Drugs, & Magick: A Journey Beyond Limits, Prometheus Rising, The New Inquisition, Reality Is What You Can Get Away With, The Walls Came Tumbling Down, Coincidance: A Head Test, Wilhelm Reich in Hell,* and *Quantum Psychology.*

NOTES

New Falcon Publications
Publisher of Controversial Books and CDs
Invites You to Visit Our Website:
http://www.newfalcon.com

At the Falcon website you can:

- Browse the online catalog of all our great titles, including books by Robert Anton Wilson, Christopher S. Hyatt, Israel Regardie, Aleister Crowley, Timothy Leary, Osho, Lon Milo DuQuette and many more
- Find out what's available and what's out of stock
- Get special discounts
- Order our titles through our secure online server
- Find products not available anywhere else including:
    - One of a kind and limited availability products
    - Special packages
    - Special pricing
- And much, much more

Get online today at http://www.newfalcon.com